Multiply YOUR BLESSINGS

Multiply YOUR BLESSINGS

A 90-Day / *Prayer Partner Experience*

August Gold and Joel Fotinos

HAMPTON ROADS

Cover design by Nita Ybarra
Cover photo by Melissa Squires
Interior designed by Dutton & Sherman Design

Hampton Roads Publishing Company, Inc.
Charlottesville, VA 22906
Distributed by Red Wheel/Weiser, LLC
www.redwheelweiser.com

Sign up for our newsletter and special offers by going to
www.redwheelweiser.com/newsletter/.

ISBN: 978-1-57174-690-0

Library of Congress Cataloging-in-Publication Data available upon request

Printed on acid-free paper in United States of America
VG
10 9 8 7 6 5 4 3 2 1

To Cat,
more precious to me than gold or silver

—AG

To Alan and Raphi, Mom and Dad, with love

—JF

ACKNOWLEDGMENTS

August and Joel wish to thank the following people for their talent and their ongoing generous support: Trace Murphy, Darya Porat, everyone at Harmony/Random House, Stephanie Kip Rostan, and everyone at the Levine Greenberg Literary Agency.

August is forever grateful for her three Prayer Partners, who enrich her life immeasurably: Her Soul Sister, Christina Wall. Her deeply creative partner, Joel Fotinos. Her brilliant friend, Doug McDonald.

Joel gives thanks to August, and to Alan and Raphi, K. Lorraine, Titi Cheryle, and Ernest—his amazing Team Family.

CONTENTS

INTRODUCTION

This book, *Multiply Your Blessings,* is not just another book about prayer. We do not give you an academic history of prayer, the possible medical benefits of prayer, a definition of the many sacred ways to pray, a theological argument or thesis about prayer, or anything of the sort.

What *Multiply Your Blessings* is, however, is a handbook for doing what the greatest spiritual masters throughout history have urged us to do: pray with one another. No less a master than Jesus gave us a clue when he urged people to "come together" in twos or threes to maximize the power of prayer. This book explains how we learned how to do that very thing, how it has worked for us and for many other people, and how you can do it as well. Practical and hands-on, *Multiply Your Blessings* is an active prayer book that you can use to magnify the power of your prayers and begin receiving more of everything you desire in your life.

Part One is an overview of what Prayer Partners are, how to go about praying together, why you should consider this practice, and what to do. Each short chapter covers a different aspect of Prayer Partnering and will answer any question you have. At the end of most of the chapters, we've included two sections. In "Think About It" we provide questions that are designed to open you up to greater possibilities regarding you and prayer and Prayer Partnering. "Try This" contains simple exercises and activities that will show you firsthand how potent prayer can be.

Along the way, you'll also read many stories about people who have used the practice of Prayer Partnering in their lives, and how it worked for them. These examples will give you ideas about what to do and how to do it. Throughout the chapters in Part One, we've also included the story of how *Multiply Your Blessings* co-author August Gold first began to pray, the amazing results she had using the Prayer Partner experience to forgive someone who had betrayed her, and what she learned along the way. For the sake of readability, Part One is written in first person, in her voice.

Part Two is "The 90-Day Prayer Partner Experience." What is it? It's a 90-day interactive workbook that you and your Prayer Partner can use to stay the course for the entire three months. There are several important sections in Part Two.

The first thing you'll see is "My Prayer Partner Commitment," which you will fill in at the start of the 90 days as a way to commit yourself to the process. After that, you'll find 90 short devotions, one for each day, that will inspire and help you along the way. Also you'll find exercises for each week of your 90-Day Prayer Partner Experience. These are tried-and-true exercises that have worked for many people and might be useful for you and your Prayer Partner. Further instruction in all of these areas will be found in the introduction to Part Two. Again for the sake of readability, we've written Part Two in first person, in Joel's voice.

There is also an appendix with a variety of prayers, and a second appendix, "The Three Secrets of Answered Prayers," taken from our earlier novel, *The Prayer Chest*. Those three secrets may have come from an earlier book, but they are excellent principles to refer to as you work with your Prayer Partner.

The aim of this book is to inspire you to try this modern version of an ancient form of prayer, one that has been used by countless millions throughout history. We want *Multiply Your Blessings* to be inspiring, fun, informative, and easy to use.

So on to the *Multiply Your Blessings* journey. As you read the book, find a Prayer Partner, and begin the process for yourself, please know that we are your Prayer Partners in spirit, cheering you on. May your Prayer Partner experience be a joyous and exciting journey.

AUGUST GOLD *AND* JOEL FOTINOS

PART ONE

Prayer Partners

If two of you agree on earth concerning anything
   that they ask,
it will be done for them by My Father in heaven.
For where two or three are gathered together in
   My name,
I am there in the midst of them.

—Matthew 18:19 –20 NKJV

1.

How Did Prayer Come into My Life?

It began innocently enough. One Sunday morning when I was in my early twenties I was reading a magazine account of a woman whose worst nightmare had come true: the small plane she was traveling in, along with her father and four other passengers, crashed in tropical, shark-infested waters. Separated from her father and the others, madly treading water in the treacherous ocean, she did something she'd never done before—she prayed. She prayed to God to help her have the strength to tread water for ten minutes, just ten minutes. And miraculously she was given the strength to keep from drowning for ten minutes. Then she prayed for another ten minutes. And she got that, too. Ten minutes by ten minutes she made it unharmed through the night one prayer at a time until she was returned safely to shore, where she was reunited with her father.

For the life of me, I could not put the magazine down. I sat hypnotized by the photographs of this woman and her father. Every single little prayer she prayed was answered, instantly. She was an ordinary woman just like me, so if she could pray and get help immediately, why couldn't I?

By the time I finished reading the article the possibility of answered prayer in my life seemed within reach. With just the belief in the *possibility*, the door that I'd closed to God years before opened. My life changed in that instant, but I didn't know it yet: I received my first answer to a prayer I did not even know I had.

Years later I would call this moment by its real name: my spiritual awakening. And it was not even my own prayer that led to my awakening—it was the prayer of the woman from the newspaper story. Nor was it my God I was praying to; she was praying to hers. I had piggybacked on the prayers of a complete stranger. Years later I would come to understand that every prayer—long or short, silent or aloud, angry or grateful, tearful or fearful—is answered through you when you are open to receive; whether it is piggybacked or stolen or counterfeit doesn't make a difference.

Prayer became a lifeline to the Divine for me, and prayer by prayer I followed in the footsteps of my heroine, one bite-size prayer at a time, until I stumbled upon the hidden truth about prayer: when we are open to receive, every prayer is answered.

So day after day I earnestly prayed the way my heroine did until one morning I hit an invisible ceiling—the more I prayed, it seemed, the less passion I experienced. I no longer looked forward to praying. I continued to speak the words correctly but they came out sounding mechanical. I wanted to feel more but I didn't. Something was missing but I didn't know what it was.

A year went by before I learned that it wasn't something that was missing but *someone*. The someone turned out to be my first Prayer Partner, Peter, who introduced me to a whole new way of praying, which changed everything.

A New Way to Pray

As it turns out, this "new" way of praying was not new at all. "If two of you agree on earth concerning anything that they ask, it will be done for them by My Father in heaven. For where two or three are gathered together in My name, I am there in the midst of them" (Matthew 18:19–20 NKJV). Jesus introduced the idea of Prayer Partnering over two thousand years ago. Every spiritual tradition has a form of praying in unison—some that predate Christianity—as a method that multiplies both the power of your prayer and its results. I didn't know that then. All I knew was that praying with someone else breathed life into my prayers in a way that nothing else had.

Suddenly I looked forward to my prayer time with my partner. It was fun and alive and utterly spontaneous. Whenever I prayed alone, I never laughed or got swept away in the excitement of connecting with the Divine. Now I was praying with fervor as I prayed with and for my partner, and he with and for me.

What to Expect from This Book

Multiply Your Blessings is a simple book about a profound spiritual technique. It is so easy that you could begin using this technique tomorrow morning and begin reaping the benefits right away. We're not inventing anything new. We're applying what Jesus taught and unleashing the power of his teaching in our own prayer lives.

Prayer Partnering changed my life forever, and it changed the life of my co-author, Joel, too. We wrote this book because we know that Prayer Partnering can do the same for you, and more.

2.

Why I Started Praying with a Partner

I'd like to report that my introduction to Prayer Partnering came after a gentle nudge from the heavens, a sweet dream from which I awoke and knew it was time for me to partner with another good soul in prayer. But it didn't happen that way. No change in my life has ever happened with a soft touch.

It is written that the "fates lead those who will, and those who won't they drag." That's me. I have to be beat up a bit to get the message that it's time to change. Then I'm all ears.

Never was that more true than when I was twenty-four years old and bought a three-story house with the love of my life. It was located in a bad neighborhood that was in the process of being gentrified, so it was only a matter of time until the value of the house increased tenfold. The plan was that we would eventually sell the house, and the money was going to support us as we grew old together.

Together we lasted two years. On the day I moved out of our house, I suggested that when the time was right, we'd need to talk about dividing the money from the sale of the house.

"Why would I do that?" Josh said coolly. "This is *my* house."

I couldn't get my mouth off the floor. This betrayal was such a shock that a year later I still had not gotten over it, let alone forgiven him. This wasn't an angry lover lashing out; clearly Josh had planned to keep the house from the day we had bought it. "Let me sign the papers for the house," he'd explained. "My bosses are conservative, and if they find out we're living together it might jeopardize my future with them. Give me your share of the money and we'll put everything in *my* name, but we both know that this is *our* house." He was studying to be a lawyer in a big Washington, D.C., law firm that was financing his education. He knew the court system inside out; it was in his blood—his father and grandfather had been lawyers. Spending time in court would be a game to him. *I had so lost the case.*

I woke up day after day dizzy with resentment and told my Judas story to anyone who would listen. Everyone agreed that Josh had stabbed me in the back, and that his was an unforgivable act. When they assured me that "what goes around comes around," I felt the sweet shiver of vindication. Their words were music to my ears.

Josh's betrayal became the central story of my life. Each day I needed to enroll more people in my point of view, so when I wasn't telling my story to some stranger I'd just met, I was revisiting the memory in my mind's eye. Most nights when I should have been sleeping I was reliving the pain of what he'd done to me. I replayed that final conversation with Josh a good five hundred times, each ending the same way in my imagination: his tear-stained humble admission that he was wrong and I was right.

On the days when the hate made it hard to breathe, I took stabs at forgiving him, mainly to have a few moments of peace, but it didn't last. Or maybe it lasted for an hour or a day, and one time even for a whole week. But then I'd return to the central premise that kept the fire of my resentment burning: a person like that doesn't deserve forgiveness. Anyway, if I forgive my betrayer, aren't I betraying myself?

The day before Prayer Partnering turned my life around, I was vacationing at a friend's house at the Delaware shore. It was a beautiful day and I was standing at the counter with the owner of a jewelry store. We were making small talk and before I knew it I was launching into the thousandth rendition of "the story."

I saw what I was doing, but I couldn't stop my anger from leaking out. When I finished I eagerly awaited the shop owner's sympathy. He looked at me with pity—not pity for what had happened to me but pity for the person I had become, an angry, bitter woman. I could see in his eyes that I was not somebody he would want as a friend. I was like the homeless man I'd seen once on the subway platform with his pant leg rolled up revealing a festering sore in hopes that someone would take pity and throw a few coins his way. The shopkeeper said the right words about how wronged I had been, but instead of feeling justified, I felt ashamed.

Awakenings, when they come, are often so subtle that if you aren't paying attention you will miss them. For a few clear moments I saw myself honestly. I saw the woman I had become by feeding my resentment of Josh: the more I blamed him, the weaker I got. I became a woman who was digging a grave for my enemy, and in the process was burying myself alive. I saw that Josh had moved on with his life and I had not.

That July night in my friend's guest bedroom I put in a midnight call to my friend Peter. He was the one who months ago had told me kindly that he was sick of listening to my sad story. He didn't mean he was sick of me, but that my story was making him sick. I was calling him because tonight I, too, was finally sick of my story. I realized that my story had sucked the life out of me over the course of the year, and I was having trouble breathing with all that hate inside me.

The conversation with Peter was short because it was late.

"Do you want to be right or happy?" he asked simply.

Who wouldn't want to be right? Yet after a year of being right, what did I have to show for it?

"Happy," I replied.

Peter asked me to tell him the last time I had been happy.

I confessed that I couldn't.

"How about the last time you were free, sweetie?" he asked kindly.

"I can't remember."

"So just forgive and let go of the story," he said, as if it were that simple.

"It's not that simple."

Peter claimed it was. "To your heart forgiveness is simple—it's only the head that has trouble with it."

"How the hell am I supposed to get from my head to my heart?" I asked, as if all this somehow were now his fault.

"You've pitched a tent in the valley of the shadow of death and have made your home there," he told me. "Don't you know the Psalm says, 'Though I walk *through* the valley of the shadow of death'? You stopped walking; I'm here to walk with you. Are you interested?"

"Who wouldn't be?"

"Okay then, for the next ninety days we will be Prayer Partners and we will pray together every morning for about five minutes." Peter said I should call him the next morning at eight. "Sharp," he added like an exclamation point, and then hung up.

Prayer What?

I had heard the familiar saying that the journey of a thousand miles begins with the first step, and I imagined that a person like me would have to walk all the way to Calcutta. But that night I got what Peter was trying to tell me about the head and the heart. The spiritual journey isn't the distance from who I am now to who I want to be; it's about moving my inner attention from my head to my heart, a distance of less than twenty-four inches. Although the distance is short, it is the most important trip we will ever be asked to take. Our head and heart, like two separate, spinning planets, are worlds apart in how they view life.

How we view life is how we do life.

I never did make it out of the rocking chair to the bed that night. As I rocked, I resented having to get up at eight and pray. I resented having to forgive my ex, who seemingly got off scot-free while I was stuck doing the work every day for three whole months. I didn't notice the blame insidiously seeping back in; when you begin with blame, there is no end to the blame.

By four in the morning forgiving felt like defeat, and by five I wished I could just wring his neck and be done with it. By six my heart was a fist.

By seven o'clock in the morning I rallied. I took a hot shower, had my coffee, and wrestled the ugly images in my head to the ground. I had read that when someone is about to die there is a last rush of life that flows through the body, like life's last stand before it is extinguished. That's what I figure happened to me that night. All of my resistance to walking through the valley of the shadow of death surfaced. The part of me that didn't want to be free of blaming Josh had its say. In letting my small, scared self emerge, I was free to make the call to my new Prayer Partner (whatever that was) and try something new.

At eight sharp I dialed Peter's number.

He never had a problem saying what he meant. "You have to really be willing to do this or you'll be wasting my time, and yours. Are you?"

When you hit bottom you can't go any lower. I said that I was ready.

"We'll be praying every morning for ninety days.

"I'll be your Prayer Partner." He told me that a Prayer Partner is different from a friend—we don't chat about things that happen in our lives. There's no talk about what our plans are for the day or chores we want to accomplish. We do just one thing together every day: pray. That's it. And we focus on each other's potential and hold the highest thoughts for ourselves and each other all throughout the rest of the day.

I told him that I could believe in the potential of my friends far more than they could believe in themselves. Peter called that "holding the High Watch" for each other. We'd pray in the morning for no more than ten minutes and then hold the High Watch for each other for the rest of the day.

"What kind of prayer?" I asked.

"Get a pen and paper. I don't know the real name of the prayer or if it ever had one, so I call it the Prayer for Forgiveness. I don't know where it came from either, but I know that it has been around forever in one form or another, and I know that it works. Write:

> For all those I have harmed, knowingly or
> unknowingly,
> I am truly sorry. Forgive me and set me free.
> For all those who have harmed me, knowingly or
> unknowingly,
> I forgive them and set them free.
> For the harm I have done to myself, knowingly or
> unknowingly,
> I am truly sorry. I forgive myself and set myself
> free.

Peter recited the prayer as if the strings of words were a string of pearls. Then he asked me to repeat the prayer with him slowly and thoughtfully, instructing me to take my time to breathe after each phrase so I could feel the prayer. As I repeated the prayer for the third time, an unexpected realization flashed through my mind: Josh wasn't my only enemy; he was one of many. Lodged in my head was a ledger sheet with the name of every person who had ever hurt me. I was dumbfounded by the length of the list.

For the rest of the day, I recited this prayer under my breath. Speaking the words for myself and for Peter was like bringing living water to my parched soul. If I didn't know better I would say that this Forgiveness Prayer was opening my heart for the first time. But how could that be when everyone knew that opening your heart, especially one as closed as mine had become, would take years of hard work? I didn't yet know that this was the result of *"where two or three are gathered together in My name."*

Each morning Peter and I shared what was happening to us spiritually, and then we prayed. I wasn't doing anything else differently in my life, so it had to be praying with Peter that was changing things. I still blamed Josh, but no longer with a vengeance. I was walking, really walking *through* the valley now. I'd become unstuck.

Peter listened but put a damper on my desire to talk through our entire prayer time. "Your prayer's not going to be answered if we spend all our time talking about it. Praying is a process that you can't force or fix or figure out, so don't analyze it to death. Let's just pray." To him prayer was everything—that's where the action was. He preferred spending every minute together praying. But there was no way I could hold in my excitement when my prayers started being answered, even if they were only teeny, tiny answers thus far. "Of course, sweetie, of course," he'd reply, as if answered prayers happened every day in his world. "Just don't forget to call me tomorrow at eight to pray—"

"And in between?" I cried, too scared to be left alone with just my prayer.

"In between I'll hold the High Watch for you."

"What are you getting out of this?"

"You'll find out that by praying for me, the answers to your prayers are multiplied. Same for me. My prayer is already being answered, just like yours."

"How did you know my prayer's already being answered, Peter?"

"How could it not be *where two or three are gathered together in My name*?" Peter wasn't a religious man, but he was a deeply spiritual man. That's what had attracted me to him in the first place. He lived in this world, all right, and paid his bills, but a part of him always was on the lookout for what life was really trying to tell him. There was the human story of his life, of what happened to him, but it was as if he turned the story upside down in search of a deeper story, the real story of how it was happening for him. To Peter nothing ever happened randomly; everything that happened was for his highest good and had a purpose. He saw everything as life talking to him about his destiny. It was from Peter that I learned one of the great truths:

***

Life is a conversation.

***

My healing began when I chose one prayer: Help me to forgive Josh. It took me on a journey that led me from my head to my heart. But first let me lay out some logistics about this powerful experience that happens *"where two or three are gathered together in My name"*—a process that we call Prayer Partnering.

Think About It

- What has your experience with prayer been? Has it been successful? Unsuccessful? Non-existent?

- What do you think prayer is?

- What does "where two or three are gathered together in My name" mean to you?

Try This

- Turn to the appendix "Prayers for Every Day," choose a prayer that speaks to you, and read it silently to yourself. How does it make you feel?

- Now go back and read it aloud. How does this feel? Does it feel more powerful reading it aloud?

- If it doesn't feel different yet, go back and read it aloud again two more times, with more feeling. Do you notice a difference?

3.

What Is
Prayer Partnering?

Here's a list of some of the things Prayer Partnering does:

- It multiplies the speed with which your prayers are answered.

- It multiplies the blessings you receive.

- It continuously builds your spiritual muscle of prayer, faith.

- It puts God first in your day.

- It opens the door to living your dream.

- It helps you grow into becoming the answer to your prayer.

- It teaches you the language of prayer.

- It opens you wider to receive the answers to your prayer.

- It teaches you the beauty of praying for others.

- It draws you more deeply into yourself and further out in life than you could if you were praying alone.

Prayer Partnering is not only about praying with someone else; it is also about engaging life in conversation and about supporting each other in having your prayers answered, your dreams realized.

In Bikram Yoga (also called Hot Yoga because it takes place in a room heated to 105 degrees) instructors tell you when you strike certain postures to "stretch continuously without intermission and without interruption." This is how you build your muscles to become both strong and flexible. The same goes for prayer. One prayer is nice, but you're not going to change your life with one prayer cried out during a crisis any more than you're going to get flexible after a single stretch. But pray continuously over the course of ninety mornings with a Prayer Partner and now you're talking.

With a Prayer Partner waiting for my call each morning I was committed to showing up. No matter how late I stayed up the night before, Peter was waiting to pray with me the next morning at eight sharp—no excuses. If I told him the day before that tomorrow would be too hectic to pray, he would ask me how serious I was about getting my prayer answered. It is one thing to say you want something and another to do the work continuously, without intermission and without interruption.

To Peter, ninety days was ninety days—not seventy, or even eighty-nine. Only ninety days of praying together would fulfill the 90-day commitment.

"Are you sure you want it?" he'd ask.

"Sure, I'm sure," I'd say, while offering an excuse for why I wouldn't be available to pray next Tuesday because I would have company staying at my apartment . . . Or the Wednesday in two weeks because I would be out of town on business . . . Or it'd be better for me if we prayed during my lunch hour, so I could sleep later in the morning. Peter must have been rolling his eyes, but all he'd ever say in reply was, "Are you serious?"

Here are two stories about being serious. Barry's story is what happens when life asks "Are you serious?" and you answer no. Paul's story is what your life looks like when you answer yes.

Barry had been a banker for the last twenty years of his life, but always beneath the surface he longed to be more creative. He'd had a dream as a boy of writing songs. Inside his pin-striped suit beat the heart of a man filled with lyrics and music. He prayed with his Prayer Partner to live his childhood dream, a dream that may have been dormant but still was very much alive! His Prayer Partner took Barry's prayer as seriously as his own, and together each morning at six-fifteen they would pray single-mindedly for both their prayers to be answered.

The moment you pray for what you want, life will challenge you. The challenge is life saying, "Are you serious?"

His partner, Kate, would end their prayer time with the same question each day. It was the last line from the poem "The Summer Day" by Mary Oliver: she'd say, "Barry, 'What do you plan to do with your one wild and precious life?'"

Within two months something marvelous opened up in Barry—he felt infused with an enthusiastic courage he'd never experienced. "I felt like a warrior ready to do battle and fight the good fight," Barry said. "That's how I used to feel as a kid—so crazy brave I'd do anything no matter how scary. All the other kids would think I was nuts, but I wasn't; I was just brave." Barry knew it was time to step out; he saw himself going into his boss's office and giving his notice. The vision empowered him. Hell, he said to himself, he had a mountain of money he had accumulated over the years, so if he wanted to take a couple of years off and discover himself, he could do so in comfort.

Then that week something happened "out of the blue." It was lunch, so the offices on his floor were half deserted. He was eating his sandwich at his desk when his boss came in. "You know, Barry," he said, "we never take the time to tell you how grateful we are for all the hard work you've done for us over the years, and we're sorry about that. I guess we're all just too busy." Barry was stunned; he sat staring wide-eyed at his boss. He couldn't remember the last time his boss had come into his office rather than summoning him, let alone spoken to him in such a warm, welcoming manner.

"We want you to have this," his boss said, pulling an envelope from his breast pocket and laying it on Barry's desk. "It's not exactly bonus time, but you can consider it a mid-year bonus. Just don't tell the others." His speech complete, he shook Barry's hand and left.

Barry was stunned when he opened the envelope and found a check for $10,000.

When we set out in the direction of a dream (which is what we do when we pray), life inevitably asks us this one all-important question: Are you serious? And Barry had yet to answer the question.

Two weeks later Barry called me. He had deposited the check in his bank account and returned with renewed zeal to work. He had stopped praying with his Prayer Partner, Kate, because his job had gotten busier and praying "was taking valuable time away from work." He was leaving for work an hour earlier in the morning. "The Prayer Partner thing was interesting," he said, "but I am too old to be fooling around with childish dreams."

Ten Great Things about Prayer

1. It works.
2. You can do it anywhere.
3. You can do it at any time.
4. You can say prayers any way you want.
5. You can pray about anything.
6. It's a great resource in difficult times.
7. It makes you more grateful.
8. It makes you happier.
9. It makes you feel more powerful.
10. You feel more connected to God.

Barry had answered life's question: he was not serious about living his dream.

Paul, on the other hand, was very serious: he had had it with working nearly sixty hours a week in real estate with no end in sight. He had no time for his wife or kids, let alone for himself. He was always running somewhere trying to keep up with his merciless work schedule. "Sure, I love the money," he admitted, "but after ten years in the biz, I get that money isn't everything if it's going to send me to an early grave." Paul had no trouble coming up with a prayer for himself: "More time to enjoy my family comfortably!" He said that he didn't want to stop working—"I'm a mess when I don't have any work to do," he confessed—"but I want to work a little, love my family a lot, and still make a great living so we can do fun things together." He prayed and then waited to see what would happen.

He didn't have to wait long before life asked him, "Are you serious?" Things at the real estate office exploded: his workload increased twofold. Now there was no time to even have his sandwich at his desk, it was that busy. "I thought, if this is the answer to my prayer, then it's the last time I'm going to pray!" Paul wasn't kidding. When the driving pace started giving him chest pains, he got the message. It was time to quit. No matter how busy it had been in his office before he prayed, quitting was never an option; now not quitting wasn't an option. He really got it, he said—he loved his family more than anything in the world. He didn't care if they wouldn't have the money for travel or vacations or a bigger house or private schools. As long as they were together, he realized, that was all that mattered. This was a real shift in perspective for him: putting the love of his family before everything. Paul had changed.

Monday morning he broke the news to his boss and returned to his desk a free man. Quitting his job wasn't the answer he had expected from his prayer, but he felt better than he'd felt in years. He'd given four weeks' notice, so while he continued to work he dreamed about all the things he would do with his family that he had never had time for. The next week his boss called him into his office. Paul thought they'd be talking logistics—severance pay, pension plan, COBRA insurance.

Instead his boss explained that he couldn't accept losing Paul. He said that he'd spent the week thinking of a way for both of them to win. This was his proposed plan: Paul could work at the office part-time, twenty hours, and in return, his boss was going to pay him for working a full-time schedule. The one condition was that Paul would not work one minute over the twenty hours agreed upon. "You could've blown me over with a feather," Paul said, laughing. "I wanted to lunge over my boss's desk and kiss him. Believe me, my boss isn't known for his generosity. This was total Divine intervention. My prayer was answered in spades. In fact I made a deal with myself that night—that I'd never ask for anything more. From then on I was just going to use my prayer time with my Prayer Partner to say thank you!"

The Tao te Ching, the Taoist philosophy of life, explains, "If you want to shrink something, you must let it grow." Life showed Barry that his love of money eclipsed his love of having a fulfilling life, and Barry chose the money. Paul learned that his love of work had eclipsed his love of his family, and Paul chose his family over the work . . . and got them both.

Think about It

- *Have you ever prayed with anyone else?*
- *What was that experience like?*
- *If it was a positive experience, list what you got out of it.*
- *If it was a negative experience, are you willing to try again?*
- *If you have had no experience, what would your ideal Prayer Partner look like?*

Try This

Turn to the appendix called "Prayers for Every Day," and choose a second prayer to read aloud beginning tomorrow morning and continuing every morning for the rest of this week, and see how it makes you feel.

4.

Which Is Better: Praying Alone or Praying with a Prayer Partner?

Praying alone and praying with a partner are as different as night and day. The former helps you grow through the miraculous power of prayer, and the latter builds you beyond what you thought you could possibly be or do by the miraculous power of praying with another consciousness steeped in Spirit.

Eastern philosophy advises us that if we want to arrive at our dream we should travel with others who are going in that direction. When we associate with like-minded people, they can

- see for us what we cannot see for ourselves,
- see our greater potential,
- see where we are hiding our greatness even from ourselves
- keep us motivated to move forward,

- inspire us by their example,
- encourage us by their belief in us,
- see the bigger picture of our talents, and
- see the whole story of who we can be when we step out of our own way.

A Prayer Partner can believe for us what we can't yet believe for ourselves. And until the time when we can believe it for ourselves, our partner is there believing it for us. Not only are they praying our biggest prayer for us, sometimes they are even carrying us in consciousness until we catch up.

Larry was stuck in a temp job, being bumped from law firm to law firm, with no chance of advancement. "Talk about a dead end," he said. "I'm going nowhere fast." So when it was time to choose a Prayer Partner he did so with great care: he chose a woman who had always believed in him. Sheryle didn't care what he was doing for a living, because she knew what Larry was capable of. For years she'd been wearing jewelry Larry had designed. Everybody thought his jewelry was brilliant; everybody, that is, but Larry. He asked Sheryle to be his Prayer Partner and of course she said yes. She'd always held a good thought for Larry, but now she would have the opportunity to formalize her good thought into prayer to lift him up, and herself along with him.

"There was no single moment when my prayer was answered," Larry said, when he spoke of his last nine months of Prayer Partnering with Sheryle. "There was no bolt of lightning from the Confidence Gods," he joked. "Just little by little every day, I got a little more confident than the day before. By the third month, I was making jewelry with the intention of maybe selling a piece or two. By the sixth month, the jewelry was selling itself through all of Sheryle's friends. At first I thought, "Well, that's Sheryle networking for me." But then the friends of Sheryle's friends started calling me and I knew it was the jewelry and my belief in it that was selling it. My belief, not Sheryle's. It's not like I'm quitting my job tomorrow," Larry said, "but my prayer I'm working toward is to support myself one day on the proceeds of my jewelry design. It's a dream come true that I am building on the shoulders of my Prayer Partner." He laughed. "You'd think I got the best end of the deal but not so . . . over the last ninety days she has lost fifteen pounds. We both scored."

I asked Larry to make the following list because he'd spent years

Ten Books with Great Prayers

1. Life Prayers *by Elizabeth Roberts and Elias Amidon*

2. Psalms for Praying *by Nan Merrill*

3. Prayer *by Ernest Holmes*

4. Prayers for Healing *by Maggie Oman*

5. Prayers to the Great Creator *by Julia Cameron*

6. This Thing Called You *by Ernest Holmes*

7. Ten Prayers God Always Says Yes To *by Anthony Destefano*

8. Illuminata *by Marianne Williamson*

9. Secrets of the Lost Mode of Prayer *by Gregg Braden*

10. Praying in Color *by Sybil Macbeth*

struggling to pray on his own but had never really gotten very far. When he'd pray alone, more often than not it was worry disguised as prayer. He couldn't lift himself up enough to have the energy and motivation and drive to pray from his highest place; he felt too low most of the time. But when he partnered with Sheryle, he found that he could climb out of his dark moods faster, and believe anything was possible. He could dream.

Praying Alone	Praying with a Prayer Partner
You pray any time you want.	You have a set prayer time in the morning.
	Working together built my discipline.
You pray for yourself.	You are praying for yourself and another.
	Praying for someone else made my heart bigger.
You hold the High Watch for yourself.	You are keeping a High Watch for yourself and another.
	I volunteered my service to my partner.
You provide inspiration.	You are inspired by each other.
	Their good inspired me to reach higher.
You receive your own answers.	We received answers for each other.
	We felt good God speaking through us both.

You are alone with Spirit.	You are in community with Spirit. *You don't feel so alone.*
You are committed to yourself.	You are committed to yourself and another. *I stopped thinking of me and began thinking of we.*
Praying alone can be isolating.	You can't hide when your partner's calling every morning *Prayer was enjoyable.*
Praying seems like something I better do or else.	You look forward to praying with your partner. *Prayer was really fun together.*
I was embarrassed to pray aloud.	I can now pray aloud for others. *Praying aloud is cool.*

Think about It

- *What benefits do you think you might receive from praying with a partner versus praying alone?*
- *How do you feel about praying every morning?*
- *How might praying with a partner every morning strengthen your faith?*

Try This

Make a list on the following page of the benefits you want to receive from praying with your Prayer Partner.

Prayer Partner Benefits

_____

_____

_____

_____

_____

_____

_____

_____

_____

_____

_____

_____

_____

_____

_____

_____

_____

Multiply YOUR BLESSINGS

5.

Prayer Partnering: What, When, Where, and How?

Adrianne was a reporter by trade and by spirit. "'What?' 'When?' and 'Where?' are the first questions I have about a story and about anything I'm expected to do," she said. "When Frank asked me to be his Prayer Partner, I shot those questions at him like bullets. I give him credit that he didn't rescind his offer then and there because I was so intense!

"It's been a while since I've been Prayer Partnering with someone else closer to home, but I still use the 'What, When, Where' method with Charlotte. I made a list of the ground rules and e-mailed it to her and then we negotiated dates and times and that was that."

Here's Adrianne's list:

What

- We are prayer partners who pray together every day for a set period of time.

- We pray for ourselves in the morning.

- We pray for each other in the morning.
- We pray for each other throughout the day.
- We pray whether it rains or shines.
- We pray whether we're in the mood or not.
- We pray whether we're sick or well.
- We pray whether we're home or out of town on business.
- We pray whether it's a busy day or a slow day.

When

- We pray every morning for 90 days in a row—no skipping.
- We pray every morning at the exact same time—no excuses.

Where

- We pray anywhere that's private—indoors or outdoors.
- We tell our family (roommates): no distractions.

How to Do It

Here's the simple Prayer Partner model that Adrianne used:

- Say hello.
- I speak my prayer aloud.

- We each briefly share a prayer update—challenges, obstacles, successes.

- You reflect my prayer back to me using my name.

- You speak your prayer aloud.

- I reflect your prayer back to you using your name.

- We take turns reading a short inspiring psalm (or reading, quote, story).

- We observe a minute of silent contemplation.

- We say good-bye.

"No dishing, no dailies, no counseling, no baloney," Adrianne says to her partner. "They know what that means—we're on the phone at this ungodly hour of the morning for one reason and one reason only: to pray, period. I don't want to hear about anything else. I laid that boundary down day one," she said, "and I've never had anyone waste my time yet." Adrianne came off tough, but she was a sweetheart. She's like one of those "tough love" sponsors in the 12-step recovery programs who is strong so your sobriety becomes strong. Adrianne takes her praying

Ten Songs to Inspire You

1. "I Believe I Can Fly" (R. Kelly)

2. "Amazing Grace" (hymn)

3. "Where There's Love There Are Miracles" (Carol Logen)

4. "Higher Ground" (hymn)

5. "Holy Now" (Peter Mayer)

6. Pachelbel's Canon

7. "Light of a Clear Blue Morning" (Dolly Parton)

8. "Beautiful" (Carole King)

9. "My God Is So Good to Me" (Rickie Byars)

10. "Only Love" (Melissa Etheridge)

seriously and she wants her partners to also. "It's the most important five minutes of my day," she confesses.

Adrianne's script doesn't have to be yours. You and your Prayer Partner have great flexibility in the way in which you choose to conduct your prayer sessions. You can also use one of the variety of prayers listed in the appendix titled "Prayers for Every Day."

Here are more ideas about Prayer Partnering:

- Prayer Partners pray once a day in the morning. Occasionally, some partners pray twice a day during a crisis situation.

- You can speak from one to fifteen minutes. No less, no more. (It will be harder to maintain a daily commitment to praying if more time than that is required.)

- You can be anywhere you want in the world and pray, including sitting side by side.

- You have to pray at least five days a week together. The other days you will be still holding the High Watch for each other.

- You can mix up the script any way that feels right to you as long as each of you prays your prayer for yourself and for the other person. There is no limit to the creative ways in which you can keep your prayer time fresh. Let your imagination be your guide.

- Include silent time. Silence connects you more deeply with yourself and each other. Without some silence it is more difficult to feel connected to Spirit.

Think about It

- Is there a place in your house where you will have privacy, where you would like to conduct your prayer time each morning? If not, can you create one?

- What is your ideal time each morning to have your 90-Day Prayer Partner Experience?

- How will being committed and consistent with your 90-Day Prayer Partner Experience improve your life?

- How many days a week do you want to commit to praying with your Prayer Partner (five, six, seven)?

Try This

Go to where you are planning to pray each morning and see if there is anything you would like to add to make it more special. Flowers? Candles? A photograph? An altar?

6.

What Are the Benefits of Prayer Partnering?

If there weren't benefits to Prayer Partnering, Jesus wouldn't have suggested it, and millions of people wouldn't be practicing it. What are some of the real benefits?

- Kath prayed for forgiveness: "I thought I'd go to my deathbed blaming my mother for how miserably she treated me as a little girl," she said. "Until I prayed with Beverly I just couldn't bring myself to forgive my mom completely. By the tenth week of praying together *I forgave my mom.* I can see that she was a sick woman and did the best she could. I'm able to remember all the wonderful things that happened when I was a kid—I could only remember the bad stuff before." Kath said that this was the first miracle of her life.

- Janet prayed for peace of mind. She said that *she could sleep through the night* now that she wasn't worrying about her husband and two kids. She hadn't realized how much lack of sleep kept her thinking fuzzy and unfocused, making her unable to make quick, clear decisions in her job.

- Hugh prayed for perfect health. He felt that after praying *he was stronger in body as well as in mind.* He said that he used to get every bug that was going around the office, and now "the bugs don't stick." His office mates are on sick leave as often as he used to be, but he hasn't missed a day of work in the last year that he has been Prayer Partnering.

- Carolyn prayed for the grace to respond calmly to situations. She told me that I wouldn't have wanted to know her before she began Prayer Partnering, because she overreacted to everything. Now, she said, she responds calmly when people cut her off in the car or get in line in front of her. *"I take a breath and respond like a normal person."*

- Bruce prayed to let go and let God. He never realized how tense he was beneath the surface, where it didn't show. His heart was always racing as he waited for the other shoe to drop. In the six months that he's been practicing Prayer Partnering, he's relaxed 70 percent. He's no longer thinking of all the bad things that could happen to him and his family. *"I'm chilled,"* he said. He turns everything over to God in the morning, and then he's free to go on with his life. Some days, naturally, are better than others.

- Manny prayed to be an open channel for financial success. He said he didn't intend to hide how much he loved material things. Since last year, when he started Prayer Partnering, he has doubled his income and moved out of the little studio he'd been living in since college. *"I've made more money in one year than I did in the five years before* put together," he said, "which is a great thing, because I'd always been an under-earner." Now he's earning what he's worth.

- Ernesto prayed to be rich. He said, "I thought I wanted to be rich when *what I really wanted was to be rich in friendships.* I made so many friends during these three months I couldn't believe it. How could I have been so lonely and never have noticed?"

- "I wanted one thing when I prayed," Mario said, "and I got it—*a green card!*" His prayer was answered. Now he is praying for a great job.

- Melissa prayed for the confidence to speak her truth. She dreamed of the day when she would be able to stand up to her boss who treated her poorly. After Prayer Partnering for six months she walked into her boss's office and told her that she couldn't treat her that way anymore. She stood up to her boss. Instead of being fired, she became her boss's personal assistant.

- Nancy prayed to love her daughter unconditionally. Nancy said she was constantly criticizing her daughter: "I'd never cut her a break. In my first month of Prayer

Partnering we had a terrible knock-down, drag-out fight," she said. "I thought I would die—we'd never fought like that. My daughter yelled at me about how we'd never really been honest with each other, never said what we needed from each other, what worked, what didn't. It was like a slap in the face, but it was the first honest talk we'd ever had. We've been friends since, and now once a week we make a cup of tea and talk about our relationship while issues are still small enough to deal with easily. *I got my daughter back*," Nancy said, smiling ear to ear.

- Craig prayed that he could learn to be accountable for his own life. "I'm not running around being a victim and blaming the world. I used to cry about all the bad things life was putting me through." Craig said.

- Lyle prayed for focus. "I was all over the place. I used to say that I had ADD because I couldn't do one thing at a time." The discipline he gained from Prayer Partnering every morning helped him to be more disciplined at work, and even to learn

Ten Psalms to Stir Your Soul

(We suggest Psalms for Praying by Nan Merrill)

1. Psalm 16
2. Psalm 27
3. Psalm 34
4. Psalm 45
5. Psalm 59
6. Psalm 110
7. Psalm 111
8. Psalm 114
9. Psalm 130
10. Psalm 132

the guitar. "It was having to show up for my Prayer Partner every morning that turned out to be the answer to my prayer."

- Steve prayed for kindness. He used to be a jerk—he was mean to everybody for no reason other than he hated himself. But feeling the love of God through his Prayer Partner was like being baptized in the healing waters of Lourdes, he'll tell you. "I'm no saint," he said, "but *I'm mellower. I like myself.* I don't want to hurt people because I'm hurting."

- Bree prayed to have a positive outlook on life. "I used to be a glass-half-empty girl," Bree said, "and now I'm a glass half full." Since she's been Prayer Partnering she's been hit with a lot of challenges that in the past she would have considered "bad," but now she sees them as opportunities to help her grow. "I don't have to defend myself against a world that's working against me. Wow," she sighs, "I'm so much more relaxed!"

Think about It

- *Do you know anybody who prays with a partner?*
- *What is their experience?*
- *What would you like to pray to have more of (e.g., more faith, more connection to others, etc.)?*
- *What would you like to pray to have less of (e.g., less worry, less fear, etc.)?*

Try This

- *Call up someone you know who has had a Prayer Partner, and ask them about their experience. What worked for them? What didn't work for them?*

- *Now that you are saying your prayer aloud each morning, add this new element: immediately after you speak your prayer aloud, spend one minute in silence. There is no wrong way to do this. Simply be silent and focus on your prayer for one minute.*

7.

How Do I Choose the Right Prayer Partner?

Choosing a Prayer Partner is not like choosing a friend or a brunch buddy. Prayer Partnering is a deep relationship; in a way it is the most intimate relationship you can have. While the connection may last for only ninety days, I know Prayer Partners who have been praying together for over six years.

And it might surprise you to find that when you're ready to pray with a partner, you will end up choosing each other.

How Do You Know You've Chosen the Right Prayer Partner?

- You feel good in their presence.
- They are upbeat, positive.
- You have important values in common.
- You share a similar vision of what life is.
- You both are interested in getting more out of life.

- You click.
- You feel that they are interested in you.
- They care about what you care about.
- They listen to you.
- They are happy for your happiness.

Nickie met her Prayer Partner volunteering at church on Sundays. She and Gavin had always gotten along great, she explained. They used to go to brunch after church and gab about everything. He loved to talk about movies and books as she did. He wasn't embarrassed to talk about how much he loved Spirit either, like some people are. Nickie was impressed with how much he loved the spiritual side of life, which was her favorite topic in the world. Her religious family never understood her love of yoga and the Eastern teachings, but Gavin did. He not only didn't judge her, he joined her in discussing such topics. He liked to listen as much as he liked to talk.

At first she thought Gavin would make a good boyfriend, but then she thought how much more important it was to have him as a Prayer Partner. At that moment in her life what she needed most was a deeper relationship with God. Having Gavin as a Prayer Partner would help her make a bigger commitment to prayer in her life. Until then she had prayed when she remembered or when things got hard. She had never thought of praying rain or shine, every morning without fail. That was a commitment to God she'd never made—putting Spirit first before everything else in her day.

It was easy for Nickie to ask Gavin to Prayer Partner with her for three months. She said that Gavin had to think about it for a few minutes—ninety days was a big commitment even if it was only for five or ten minutes a morning. "He told me that Prayer Partnering would mean that our relationship was going to go to another level," Nickie said, "and that he had to decide if he wanted that." Nickie knew she did. She knew Prayer Partnering would make them closer spiritually, and she looked forward to having that closeness with someone. Until that time she had just seen people at church on Sundays and then not at all during the week. She felt as if she was walking her spiritual path all by herself. She felt isolated. She knew that Prayer Partnering was the first step to making a bigger commitment spiritually to someone she trusted.

When Gavin smiled and said yes, she jumped up and hugged him; she couldn't help it. She knew it was the beginning of something "bigger than we were."

I saw Nickie at church a few months back and she had an engagement ring on her finger.

Ten Qualities of an Ideal Prayer Partner

1. Trustworthy
2. Compassionate
3. Nonjudgmental
4. Kind
5. Sense of humor
6. Positive outlook
7. Spiritually connected
8. Empathetic
9. Inspiring
10. Committed

She was beaming. She and Gavin had become engaged after being Prayer Partners for a year and a half. When she prayed for love, she confessed, she never dreamed it would be Gavin who answered her prayer.

In Gavin, Nickie found the qualities that were right for her:

- He loved Spirit.
- He loved to talk.
- He shared her interests in movies and books.
- He shared her love for the Eastern spiritual teachings.
- He loved to volunteer and be of service to others.
- He didn't judge her for her choices.
- He had a positive outlook on life.

"Tell everybody," she said, "that this stuff really works." I said I would.

Think about It

- *What qualities do you have that a Prayer Partner would find appealing?*
- *How are the qualities you'd look for in a Prayer Partner different from what you would want in a friend? Or are they the same?*

Try This

- List any other qualities you did not find on the lists in the preceding pages but that are important to you in choosing a Prayer Partner.

- Review your list of qualities and the lists of qualities in the preceding pages, and choose the top ten qualities that you would find appealing in a Prayer Partner. Write your list below.

The Qualities I Want in a Prayer Partner

_____

_____

_____

_____

_____

_____

_____

_____

_____

_____

_____

_____

_____

_____

_____

_____

8.

Where in the World Will I Find a Prayer Partner?

Prayer Partnering is a spiritual experience.

Now that you know your Prayer Partner doesn't have to be anyone extra-religious or even religious at all (if that's not who you are), you don't have to limit your search to churches and synagogues. You can meet a Prayer Partner wherever you are. If you are in the right spirit, you will attract them.

Potential Prayer Partners can be found anywhere. Here are some examples:

The Greek root of the word "spiritual" means "to breathe." A Prayer Partner is someone to pray with so that you can both breathe more deeply in your lives . . . into your lives.

- Steve met his Prayer Partner in his circle of friends.

- Karen met her Prayer Partner at the gym—her fitness trainer.

- Lucy met hers in her weekly book discussion group.

- Jan met hers while volunteering for Race for the Cure.

- Larry met his in his monthly off-road bike club.

- Sean chose her librarian as her Prayer Partner.

The number of places where you might come in contact with a person who'll make a perfect Prayer Partner is endless. The list includes your friends who live near you or those who live out of town. It could be your neighbor, a member of the co-op board, a co-worker, a fellow student, or someone sitting next to you in the library. It could be your butcher, baker, or candlestick maker. It could be the parents of your daughter's best friend or your mechanic at the garage. The list is endless.

Ten Places to Meet a Prayer Partner

1. Church, synagogue, or spiritual group
2. Through a friend
3. Already a friend
4. Someone you admire
5. Book club
6. Neighbor
7. Business associate
8. 12-step recovery group
9. Gym
10. Social group (biking, cards, knitting, etc.)

Think about It

- *Are there people in your life who have the qualities you want in a Prayer Partner?*

- *Note: If you don't have someone in your life yet who would make a good Prayer Partner, don't worry. Now that you have the intention to find one, you will find one or they will find you. Keep in mind that your prospective Prayer Partner might be different from what you might imagine.*

Try This

If there are some people in your life who have the qualities you are looking for in a Prayer Partner, make a list of their names on the following page.

Prospective Prayer Partners

_____

_____

_____

_____

_____

_____

_____

_____

_____

_____

_____

_____

_____

_____

9.

What Do I Pray For?

It's great to pray for world peace, and for more enlightened world leaders and governments with heart, but after twenty years of being a minister and praying with tens of thousands of people, I've learned that when we pray to heal ourselves, the world around us is healed.

At every Sunday service at my spiritual center the congregation recites the following Peace prayer:

Peace in my heart brings peace to my family. Peace
in my family brings peace to my community. Peace
in my community brings peace to my nation.
Peace in my nation brings peace to my world.

*Let there be peace
on earth and let it
begin with me.*

The world is in such bad shape, we think. We better do something fast. We think that when the world gets better, so will we. The truth is just the opposite:

"As within, so without," the Hermetic Law states.

When we get better, so does the world around us. The world's peace depends on the peace in our heart; the world's wholeness depends on our own.

There is a story about a little boy who is sent to detention for acting out during his geography class. As a punishment, his teacher takes a map of the world and tears it into small pieces. She gives it to him and tells him that he cannot leave the detention room until he has put the map back together again.

"As within, so without," the Hermetic Law states.

The little boy thinks that there's no way he can accomplish this task even if he spent all week on it, yet one short hour later he hands the patched-up map back to his teacher.

She is flabbergasted. "How did you do this?"

"It was easy," he said. "I turned all the pieces over and on the other side there was a picture of a torn man. When I put the whole man together and turned the paper over, the world was whole again, too."

So take your eyes off the problems of the world for a moment and place them squarely on yourself, and ask this question: "Where am I stuck?"

Where you are stuck is what you are going to pray for.

Why Should I Focus My Prayer on the Places Where I'm Stuck?

- It will make the biggest difference in your life.

- It will free up a great deal of physical and emotional energy.
- You will feel better about every other area of your life.
- You will breathe more deeply.
- You will sleep better.
- You will feel more positive about your life.

We do not realize the real price we pay by being stuck in our lives. I didn't. I thought it was no big deal; I could handle it—as long as it didn't show, I had it under control.

If you have to control something in your life, it's already out of control.

I already told you that my first Prayer Partner experience was about forgiveness, and I was not a woman who forgave easily. When Josh betrayed me by stealing from me, I assumed I'd go to my grave with that grudge. All grudges have real beginnings: someone does something bad to you and you are innocent and they are guilty. The problem with being stuck in a grudge is that grudges grow and turn into full-time obsessions that take over your life. Your rightness and their wrongness become a daily fever, and you spend your time trying to enroll others in the story of what happened to you. That's where I got stuck. I couldn't forgive, I couldn't let go of the story, and when I got stuck there, every other area of my life got stuck, too.

They say that how you do one thing is how you do everything, and to me that's what happened when I closed the door of my heart to Josh. My head said that I had closed my heart with good reason, but good reason or no, at the end of the day a closed door in me was still a closed door, and nothing new could come in. My job was relocating south and I wasn't making the move, which meant I was about to be out of a job. I was living in a city that brought out the worst in me; and I was living, or should I say surviving, from paycheck to paycheck. My heart was a closed fist, and my tight little life reflected that.

Because "stuck" is a concept that we can't see; we think it's no big deal, but being stuck does immense damage below the surface. If we could see what stuck looks like, we'd pray like mad to get unstuck first before we prayed for anything else. Not more than a week or two after I started Prayer Partnering with Peter, I got to see what being stuck looks like. Once I got the visual, I never questioned the insidious danger of letting myself stay stuck in any area of my life for too long until this happened.

I had always chosen plants that required the barest minimum of care because that's what I knew I could provide. Most of them hung in there. However, one was neglected to the extent that its roots were practically exposed on the surface of its sparse soil. My first thought was to transplant it sometime later, maybe over the weekend, but then I'd said this very thing for months, which is why it was now struggling to survive. I decided to be a bit late for work and transplant it so I wouldn't come home to a dead plant that night.

I had a couple of spare ceramic pots beneath my sink left over from former plants that hadn't made it. Each pot was about two sizes bigger than the pot the plant was currently in. I figured this would give the plant plenty of room to grow. I set out newspaper on the kitchen counter and got to work quickly trying to release the plant from its current container. I gently tugged but it wouldn't budge. I tugged more firmly but still nothing. I stepped up the pressure until I knew that if I tugged any harder I'd break the plant in two. What was up with this damn plant!

What I hadn't expected was how stuck the plant was in the current pot, which it had apparently outgrown long ago. The plant wasn't going to budge and I had to get to my job, so I took the hammer out of my tool drawer and softly cracked the clay pot into three pieces.

Ten Great Things to Pray for (Other Than Money)

1. Health
2. Happiness
3. Joy
4. Clarity
5. Peace of mind
6. Patience
7. Love
8. Meaningful work
9. Great friends
10. Contentment

I'd heard the word "root-bound" and even used it cavalierly once or twice in conversation, but I never knew what a root-bound plant looked like. Right before my eyes I saw how the roots of the plant were wound round and round, the plant literally strangling itself to death below the surface of the soil. No matter how much sunshine or plant food or water I had given it, it wouldn't have been able to grow in this pot that was too small for it.

Praying every morning improved my ability to see the meaning of things that I previously wouldn't have given a second thought to. In front of me I saw myself as the plant choking on the roots of blame and the unwillingness to forgive. Sure, I told people at work that I was fine. I could lie to others about how I was on the outside. But underground, in the darkness of our heart and soul, we can't lie; we can only tell the truth. Even if we deny it or run away from it or lie to ourselves about it, deep down inside, the truth about what we're doing to ourselves is waiting.

Even if I won the lottery and didn't have to lift a finger at a job or pay a mortgage or do anything I didn't want to do in my life, I would never be happy or free. There would be no life for this plant or for me until I'd freed the plant from its smaller pot, unwound the roots from around the plant, and transplanted it in new soil in a much bigger pot where it could grow. The hammer turned out to be my Prayer Partner. The bigger pot was what I prayed for every day for ninety days.

Think about It

- *In what area(s) of your life do you feel stuck?*

- *How long have you been stuck in this area (or these areas)?*

- *What would be different in your life if this area (or these areas) was no longer an issue?*

Try This

On the following lines, make a list of what you would like to pray for. Circle the one that is most important for you right now.

What I Would Like to Pray For

_____

_____

_____

_____

_____

_____

_____

_____

_____

_____

_____

_____

_____

_____

_____

10.

How Do I Pray?

Nearly a decade ago I was introduced to a very easy way to create powerful, positive prayers. The prayers I began creating bore no resemblance to the prayer of my childhood that had me begging or beseeching some faraway Source in the hopes that It would hear my pleading and give me something I didn't have. The beauty of this newer method is in how easy it was to construct a prayer that empowers you as you speak it. Your prayer looks like this:

The name for the Source . . .
where the Source dwells . . .
your heart's desire . . .

The Name for the Source

In the first part of the prayer you insert the name of the God of your understanding. "Of your understanding" means that however you understand the Source of Life is right and true for you. Don't let the word "God" stand in the way of your having a connection with the Source.

Personally, I'm comfortable with any of the following names:

- Spirit
- Infinite Life
- The Eternal Tao
- The Ground of All Being
- Life
- Great Mother
- Divine Mother/Father
- Great Unity
- God
- The Hidden Creator
- Creator
- Absolute Reality
- Divine Mind
- The Absolute
- The One
- The Source of Life
- Divine Love
- The Living Presence

There are thousands of names for the Divine, all of them right and true for the person speaking them. You need only concern yourself with the names for the Presence that make It personal for you, so you feel connected to It, in relationship with It. This takes the relationship out of your head and places it in your heart. Remember, we breathe life into our prayers with our feelings.

And relationships start in our heart with how we feel about the thing we are relating to.

Spirit is not a concept we learn—it is a relationship we have.

Where the Source Dwells

In the second part of the prayer you identify where this Source dwells in relationship to you so that you can further deepen your connection to it. In this part of the prayer you fill in where you will find this Source of Life. Where does the Source of Life dwell? Examples are:

- Within and around all things
- Within me
- Within and around me
- Moving within me
- Moving through me
- Expressing itself as me
- Flowing through me
- Indwelling

Your Prayer Request, or Your Heart's Desire

In part three of the prayer in present tense you write what it is your heart desires, or your prayer request. What do you need or want?

- Health
- Creative flow
- A better job
- Clarity

- Peace of mind
- Freedom from debt
- To love myself

When you put the three parts together, your prayer will sound like this:

- Divine Mother/Father within me heals me now.
- One Mind that is my mind now clears the way for new ideas.
- Holy Spirit that lives in my heart and soul frees me from my addiction.
- The Tao flowing through me leads me to my true love.
- God living in and through me guides me to my perfect job.
- Divine Love indwelling frees me to love myself.
- My Lord, which is my very life, shows me how to love myself.
- Christ Consciousness, which is my consciousness, makes me strong in body.
- Absolute Truth expressing as me unleashes my creativity.

As you pray for each other, simply take the prayer and speak it for your Prayer Partner:

- Divine Mother/Father within James heals James now.
- One Mind, which is James's mind now, clears the way for new ideas.

- Holy Spirit, which lives in James's heart and soul, frees him from his addiction.
- The Tao flowing through James leads him to his true love.
- God living in and through James guides him to his perfect job.
- Divine Love indwelling frees James to love himself.
- The Lord, which is James's very life, shows him how to love himself.
- Christ Consciousness, which is James's consciousness, makes him strong in body.
- Absolute Truth expressing as James unleashes his creativity.

When you speak the prayer for yourself and for your Prayer Partner in the morning or throughout the day, you're breathing life into it. We are instructed to "Love the Lord your God with all your heart, with all your soul, and with all your strength." Let this be the way in which we pray—with the fullness of our whole heart. These are living words that are creating the life you desire, so feel the life force moving through them. Bring them to life with your excitement and passion and joy, so that not only can you feel yourself praying, but you can feel yourself receiving the answer to your prayer. Don't be afraid to repeat your prayer aloud many times until you can feel it "take root within your very own heart."

The most effective prayers are short and sweet. Pray for one thing at a time. You should be able to memorize your prayer the first day, as should your Prayer Partner. A dozen words is plenty for a prayer; any more than that is too much.

Our fear, of course, is that if we don't say everything we want, or leave out anything, we won't get what we want. Of course this is foolishness. Divine Mind, which is dwelling in and through us, knows what we need before we ask. How many times did Jesus assure us of this? Prayer is less about outlining for God what we desire than knowing it for ourselves—knowing we deserve it, knowing we're worthy of having it, and being willing to open to receive it. (For a full explanation of the three secrets of answered prayers, see Appendix B.)

Ten Timeless Names for God Other Than God

1. Spirit
2. I Am
3. The Divine
4. Creator
5. Lord
6. One Mind
7. The Infinite
8. Source
9. Beloved Friend
10. Living Presence

Think about It

- *Do you have a relationship with God? If so, what has your relationship with God been like?*

- *How were you taught to pray as a child? Did it work?*

- *How do you pray now? Does it work?*

Try This

- *Make a list of the names for God that you love. (Choose names from the list provided on the preceding pages, or make your own list.)*

- *Then make a list of where you believe the Source dwells in relationship to you.*

- *Copy both of those lists onto the next page and circle the item from each list that speaks to you most strongly right now.*

My Favorite Names for God

_____

_____

_____

_____

_____

_____

_____

_____

_____

_____

_____

_____

_____

_____

_____

Where the Source Dwells

_____

_____

_____

_____

_____

_____

_____

_____

_____

_____

_____

_____

_____

_____

_____

_____

_____

_____

My Prayer Request

_____

_____

_____

_____

_____

_____

_____

_____

_____

_____

_____

_____

_____

_____

_____

_____

11.

Should I Memorize My Prayer?

I'm a strong advocate for memorizing. In ancient times all truth teachings were repeated until the student memorized them. When you memorize a prayer, it is yours; it is no longer the author's. You can now claim it because it is in you and you can call it forth at any moment you wish. It's in your body and your mind and your soul. It is there whenever you need it. Those words of truth have power when you call them forth and speak them—real power. It's a different story when you have to hunt for a book and turn to the right page and then read the words from the page. That kind of prayer is a prayer that is not in you or of you. It's not yours but someone else's.

Maya Angelou tells a story of when she was a young woman and her teacher, Frederick Wilkerson, asked her to speak the single line "God loves me," taken from the book *Lessons in Truth* by Emilie Cady. Maya spoke the words mechanically, as if the words didn't apply to her. She knew they were supposed to be true, but she didn't feel as if they were true for her.

So her teacher asked her to repeat that statement of truth aloud one more time. "God loves me." She might as well have been reading from the phone book for all the feeling she put into that statement. "Again," the teacher instructed. "God loves me." She repeated the words that still meant nothing to her.

"Again."

Again Maya Angelou repeated, "God loves me." And again. And again. And she found herself without his prompting repeating the words, "God loves me . . . God loves me . . . God loves me . . ."

Unbeknownst to her, after the seventh repetition, immersing herself in this statement of truth, the words were no longer words; they began taking root inside her heart. Each time, she repeated the sentence with a little bit more feeling. "God loves me . . ." blossomed into a feeling of love that she'd never felt before. "God loves me, me, Maya Angelou, *me*."

Ten Great Poems to Uplift You

1. "Why I Wake Early," Mary Oliver
2. "Love After Love," Derek Walcott
3. "Last Night as I Was Sleeping,"Antonio Machado
4. "Lake and Maple," Jane Hirshfield
5. "Sweet Darkness," David Whyte
6. "The Guest House," Rumi
7. "The Long Boat," Stanley Kunitz
8. "The Journey," Mary Oliver
9. "All I Was Doing Was Breathing," Mirabai
10. "You See I Want a Lot," Rainer Maria Rilke

God loved her! She felt that love, she believed in it, and she realized that if God loved her, anything was now possible. Now the truth wasn't just true; it was true for *her*.

When you take your prayer into your mind, take it even deeper into your heart. It is the feeling of the heart that breathes life into your prayer.

Your feelings provide the fire of desire that gives life to your prayers.

Maya Angelou couldn't feel the love of God by saying those three words, "God loves me." But when she said them repeatedly and said them from her heart, and felt what those words meant, then the prayer began to come to life. Then the prayer she was speaking began to be answered.

You have to enter more deeply into the prayer until you can feel the life force hidden within it. If a prayer is a living thing, then it is you who is going to give it its life. It's you who has to breathe life into it. It's you who has to feel the thrill of your answered prayer, not as some future thing, but as a present reality. "God loves me," not next year, or even in the next minute, but right here and right now.

The answer to the prayer is in the prayer itself.

Memorizing your prayer allows you to turn off your critical mind as you do when you're listening to music or singing a familiar song, where the words and melody arouse your heart. You feel the music; it moves you. The music lifts you out of yourself. It is the same with a prayer. It is music to your heart, the psalm of your soul. It is a poem, a love song, your heart's desire. But if you say it without feeling, it is not alive.

Think about It

- *Have you ever committed anything to memory (a song, a poem, a spiritual law)?*

- *How has that helped you?*

Try This

Read your prayer aloud with your Prayer Partner every morning. Throughout the day, repeat the prayer to yourself silently as often as you remember, so you keep it alive in your heart and mind.

12.

What Might I Feel When I Start Praying with a Prayer Partner?

When you are praying together you might be surprised by the unexpected feelings that might emerge. It's perfectly natural. If we are the channel through which our prayer is answered, then whatever is blocking that channel has to surface so we can deal with it and release it. Once it is released, we are open to receive the answer to our prayer.

Here are some stories of people who entered the process of "where two or three are gathered together in My name."

- Lara said she felt *guilty* because she was raised in a home where her family didn't believe in prayer. Her parents thought praying was for people who were weak, so in some way by praying she felt that she was betraying her parents' beliefs.

- Megan was just plain *scared*. She knew about praying in church but didn't know how to feel about praying with someone else. It was so personal.

- Pat *hates getting out of bed* in the morning to pray, period.

- Jack said praying made him feel *weak*. Why wasn't he strong enough to solve his own problems without begging for help? Isn't that how his father did it?

- Larry felt mortified at the thought that his friends might find out that he was praying every morning. He never told anyone what he was doing; he was too *embarrassed*.

- Pamela gets butterflies every morning before calling her Prayer Partner. *She's afraid her prayer won't be answered.*

- Monica is *afraid her prayer will be answered* before she's ready.

- Zoe *feels like she's wasting time*; she thinks she'd get more things done if she didn't have to spend the first ten minutes of her day praying.

- Rachel is *afraid she might lose her material things* because she is focusing so much on spiritual things now.

- Brenda is scared that praying every day might make her too religious for her friends and *they won't like her anymore.*

- Dan can't shake the feeling that he's *not good enough*: "I still drink and have a lot of girlfriends and am not always as honest as I should be."

- Nothing in his past prepared Stanley for praying with someone. Prayer Partnering made him feel *inadequate*, like he was doing it wrong.

On the other hand, here are people who have experienced joy in Prayer Partnering:

- Seana couldn't believe how *relieved* she felt not having to carry the burden of her healing all by herself, as she did with everything else in her life.

- Nancy felt *confident*. To know that God was her first stop every morning gave her a confidence she'd never felt before.

- Alicia felt *"like a million bucks."* "How cool to connect with the Divine before I go swim with the sharks at work," she said. "To know that I'm all prayed up before I leave my house makes me feel like I can deal with anything that comes up."

- Clara used to start her day with the morning news shows and the *New York Times.* By the time she was done with the "news" she was a wreck. "Now I start my day by knowing the truth," she said. "Wow, I'm another woman—calm and *centered in the truth of who I am.* I'm not nervous all the time." Clara is most proud of having flushed her anti-anxiety medication down the toilet!

- "I used to be so afraid of dying," Vinny, a senior citizen, admitted. "Now I'm *so focused on living I don't have time to worry about dying.*"

- Jane felt *the presence of Spirit* with her throughout the day. Prayer Partnering was an invitation to God to walk with her hand in hand. She had never felt so close to God before in her life.

- Brian said *Prayer Partnering made God real for him.*

- Tom's biggest accomplishment is getting out of bed before noon without a hangover. He no longer stays out all night drinking; he has an important commitment to Spirit every morning, and he hasn't missed a morning yet. Praying gives his day a *higher purpose and meaning* than just "dragging my ass through the day."

- Bree had a telephone book filled with friends but n*ever got closer with anyone than she did with her Prayer Partner.* "Nobody's got my back like my Prayer Partner does," she said.

- "Starting my day by letting God love me," Jonathan said, "has *made me love myself more.*"

- "I feel like I'm *no longer alone spiritually,*" Frank said.

Ten Ideal Places to Pray

1. By water
2. Park
3. Museum
4. Nature walk
5. In front of your altar
6. Comfortable couch
7. Meditation corner/room
8. Outdoors
9. Garden
10. Any place private and quiet

For a middle-aged man who has felt alone his whole life, that's a miracle.

- Darla *doesn't get distracted* by the hundreds of chores on her to-do list anymore now that she's got her priorities straight. Since she made prayer the first priority in her life—first thing every morning—all her other responsibilities have fallen into place. By taking the ten minutes in the morning for God, she has more than enough time for everything else she needs to do.

The moral of all these stories is that it doesn't matter what you feel, because by the time you reach the end of the ninety days you'll have experienced dozens of different feelings. Prayer Partnering grows you into becoming the answer to your prayer, and that means you're going to have some growing pains. Whatever you feel, feel it, and don't judge it. Let what wants to emerge, emerge, and then let it go. You're just opening the channel through which you'll be receiving the answer to your prayer.

Think about It

- *Is there a special date on which you would like to start the 90-Day Prayer Partner Experience?*
- *Why that date?*
- *How do you think it might feel praying with another person every day (e.g., awkward, embarrassing, exciting, etc.)?*

13.

What Can I Expect from Prayer Partnering?

You can expect some of the following things to happen as you begin praying with your Prayer Partner:

- The answer to your prayer rarely looks like what you think it's going to look like.

- Prayer doesn't change the world; it changes you. Only when you change can the world around you change.

- Every answer to your prayer helps you expand until you become open enough to receive the answer to your prayer.

- Attracting the answer to your prayer and holding it are two different skill sets. The answer to your prayer comes to fruition when you can successfully hold what it is you are praying for.

- Some answers to your prayer may direct you to inner obstacles you need to overcome in order to move forward.

For example, my first Prayer Partnering experience was about *forgiveness*. I did nothing but focus on forgiving for ninety days. By the second month (which felt like the second year) I felt my resentment toward Josh waning, but I sure wasn't awash in the milk of human kindness when I thought about him. I was far, far away from forgiving him. I learned that it takes at least ninety days for real change to take root.

Thankfully I had Peter as a Prayer Partner, because otherwise I might have thrown in the towel after a month. But he kept me on track; I felt accountable to holding his prayer, for keeping the High Watch for him. That kept me going, especially when I bumped into a memory of someone else whom I hadn't forgiven. While my ex-boss's betrayal wasn't nearly as bad as what Josh had done to me, just the thought of him made my stomach clench into a ball. I hadn't thought of him for a while, but there he was—living inside me in some dark corner, sucking the love right out of me. It seemed the more I prayed for forgiveness, the more people I remembered I had to forgive.

This is the genius of Prayer Partnering, and also the pain in the neck: instead of my forgiveness list shrinking, during my ninety days it kept growing, and I added my ex-boss to the list. I remember my conversation with Peter clearly:

"What? I'm supposed to forgive him and just like that he's off the hook?"

"No, just like that *you* are!"

I had worked for this "S.O.B." for a year. It's important to know that he was hated by everyone in the company, not just by me. I, however, held a special kind of dislike for him because I was employed as his personal assistant, his right-hand gal, which meant that because I was within striking distance I got the bulk of his abuse. He was a sour human being who took his unhappiness out on everyone around him. I stuck with it because I needed the job.

My boss was my enemy. All the great teachers, unfortunately, give us the same advice about dealing with our enemies. Jesus said we need to "love our enemies." Name something harder than that! The Tao te Ching goes further in verse 69: "There is no greater misfortune than feeling 'I have an enemy.' For when 'I' and 'enemy' exist together there is no room left for my treasure." Our treasure is lost. That's why forgiveness is not a luxury but a necessity: we don't forgive our enemies for their sake, but for our own, so we don't turn out to be sour human beings who belittle and diminish others.

Everything is connected, Chief Seattle and the modern day physicists tell us. "Whatever we do to the web of life," Chief Seattle explained, "we do to ourselves." It's a simple formula: if I don't set my enemy free, then I'm not free.

My boss from hell was sitting across the table from me. This was the first lunch he'd invited me to in my year with him; I knew it was anything but social. He was too mean to be social. At his insistence I wore a beeper hung around my neck and he beeped me more often than one would think humanly possible in a ten-hour workday. I was more slave than personal assistant; there was seemingly no end to the work. I swore that I was doing the work of two people on his behalf, and still my efforts never merited a simple thank-you. This is to say that I'd rather have been lost at sea in a rubber raft in the middle of the Indian Ocean than be at lunch with this man.

His smile threw me off my guard. "How are you liking your job?" he asked kindly.

It had to be a trick question. "Wow," I said, "it's been quite a year." I didn't mention that when he hired me I was smoking one pack of cigarettes a day, and now, with the stress of working for him, I was smoking two.

"I hope you mean 'wow' in a good way. Are you liking the work?" His voice was gentle, his eyes friendly; this was a different man.

Maybe he had changed? Maybe this was the real him?

So I told him the truth. "'Wow,' as in it's quite a busy job," I confessed, smiling back at him.

"Too busy?" he asked, giving me his full attention, as if nobody existed in this restaurant but the two of us.

"Can I be honest?" I asked.

"Of course. That's why I wanted to get us out of the office, so we could be frank with each other."

If this was a trap, I couldn't see it. "Well, if you want to know the truth, the sheer volume of work is overwhelming." His eyes widened in sincere concern, beckoning me to continue.

"I feel like I'm doing the work of two people."

He had no idea, he said. If he'd only known, he said. He said many things that led me to believe that speaking my truth was a smart move. Maybe he'd lighten my workload? Maybe he'd give me a raise? I was beginning to feel that if things came up between us in the future I wouldn't be afraid to tell him how I felt. I could be honest. I was relieved.

He thanked me for my honesty, paid the bill, and we returned to the office and my mountain of work.

Two days later, in a sentence containing less than a dozen words, he fired me. Effective immediately. He sent the head of human resources, Karen, who was to help me pack and escort me out of the building. She had the wages owed me in a check in her hand.

When my boss returned to his office and slammed the door behind him, a habit we all hated, Karen let out a breath. Apparently she couldn't breathe around him either. "You know," she said, "up until you came, this job was held by

Ten Surprising Things to Be Grateful For

1. Being alive
2. Your favorite song
3. Dinner at your favorite restaurant
4. A check in the mail
5. Candlelight bath
6. A great book to curl up with
7. A decadent dessert
8. An unexpected trip out of town
9. An old friend from your past contacting you
10. A random act of kindness

two women. He fired them both for not working hard enough, and then he replaced them with you."

"I knew it—"

She shushed me, obviously as intimidated by my boss as I was.

I whispered to her as I emptied my desk, "I told him that it felt like I was doing the work of two people."

"Don't feel bad. It wouldn't have mattered what you told him. I've been with him for ten years and he's never changed. The people around him do, though: the brave ones quit; the rest he fires. It's a revolving door."

"And which are you?" I asked.

"I'm a glutton for punishment," she said. "He reminds me of my father. I must think that if I can make peace with him it'll be like making peace with my father. Crazy, right?"

I was still smoking back then and I opened a new pack of cigarettes and offered her one, her first of the day, she said. My twenty-first. My tears began flowing, but they were tears of relief.

"Believe me," she said, "he did you a favor."

This Prayer Partnering had a way of stirring up old unwanted memories that were better left dead and buried. But the problem was that while the memories might have been buried, they weren't dead. I'd buried them alive and they were coming back to haunt me. My boss stood in the way of forgiving Josh, and Josh stood in the way of my moving forward in my life.

What choice did I have but to pray for the willingness to forgive them? And as I did I hoped that no more skeletons were going to come out of the closet looking for forgiveness. But of course I knew they would because it was still only month two of Prayer Partnering and I wasn't free yet.

I was seeing a bit more clearly how this process worked: I prayed for a certain intention, and as long as I dealt with everything that Life brought me, I moved one step closer to opening to receive the answer to my prayer. I might not have liked the process—I'd much rather have had my prayer answered in twenty-four hours and be done with it—but I understood the logic of it, and dare I add, the beauty.

Think about It

- *What do you expect might happen during this 90-Day Prayer Partner Experience?*

- *How might this experience change you in a positive way?*

- *What things about yourself would you like to have change?*

14.

What Are the Prayer Partnering Do's and Don'ts?

The difference between Prayer Partnering and other forms of get-togethers is that this prayer time has nothing to do with the busy comings and goings of our daily lives. This is a time when the focus is entirely on the greater story of our lives, our spiritual lives. These few minutes together each morning are food for our soul, which will then inform the rest of our day at work and play in the world. When the Bible says someone has "climbed the mountain," it is an invitation for *us* to climb the mountain of consciousness with our partner, looking at our lives from a higher perspective. From this elevated height we become larger than our daily concerns. From this height we can't see the details; instead the beautiful whole of our lives is revealed. When we look at our daily problems from this height, the ones that seem so big—the ones that often take up all of our attention—have gotten smaller as we've grown larger.

From this height we see what riches are really important in life: love, meaningful work, knowing the truth of who we are, why we're here, and fulfilling our personal destiny. This is what the prayer time is for—connecting with the essential miraculous wonder of our lives, and the Spirit of Life Itself. With this enlarged perspective, we are enlarged; and with our enlarged self we turn back to our daily lives—more centered and connected, clear-sighted and calm. Less fearful. We're breathing more deeply, taking life in. We are open to receive all of life's riches.

We take our sacred mountaintop experience with us into our day and everything we touch becomes sacred.

A lot of what you will find in the following do's and don'ts lists is commonsense, like adhering to the strictest confidentiality, listening with your full attention, and removing all distractions during your few minutes of prayer time.

Ten Qualities You Like Most about Yourself

1. Curious
2. Intelligent
3. Survivor
4. Great friend
5. Unique
6. Does the right thing
7. Inspiring
8. Giving
9. Loving
10. Spiritual

Do's

- Listen.
- Be open.
- Keep everything that is said confidential.
- Keep your mind centered on Spirit.

- Speak your prayer in the present tense.
- Look at everything through the lens of it happening you.
- Start on time/end on time.
- Be prepared for prayer time.
- Pray in a quiet, uninterrupted space with no distractions.
- Share the spiritual experience that you are going through.
- Focus on your partner's strengths.
- Put a stop to all talk that doesn't belong in the prayer time: this is a time to focus on the spiritual story only.

Don'ts

- Don't engage in small talk.
- Don't criticize your Prayer Partner.
- Don't judge.
- Don't gossip.
- Don't complain.
- Don't bring your problems into the prayer time.
- Don't discuss your daily chores, your to-do list.
- Don't try to fix the other person.
- Don't focus on the problem.

- Don't counsel or give advice.

- Don't do problem solving.

- Don't unload your personal/professional troubles.

- Don't text, answer e-mails, watch TV, cook, or make coffee during your prayer time.

Remember

- You are Prayer Partners only, not counselors or advisers.

- This is sacred work that you are involved in.

- While you might be in your living room or kitchen, you are both gathered together in the name of the Most High, and as such you are standing on holy ground.

Think about It

- *Are you a good listener?*

- *Look over the do's and don'ts lists. Where do you recognize yourself in either list?*

Try This

Make your own do's and don'ts lists of what you want this Prayer Partner experience to be like—that is, what will work for you and what won't work for you. Compare this list with your Prayer Partner's list.

15.

How Do I Keep My Prayer Partnering Fresh?

Mia had been praying with her partner, Neal, for five months. They talked every morning at the same time and prayed in the same way. "I mean, we're even praying the same prayer from day one." One morning she blurted out, "I'm bored!" Neal was relieved because as it turned out so was he. He hadn't wanted to say anything because he didn't want to hurt her feelings. Once the topic was broached they began to mix up their Prayer Partnering to make it more fun. "Why isn't our prayer time fun when we're such fun people?" Mia exclaimed.

Neal was willing to take some of the blame. "Prayer in my family was done in a solemn whisper," he said. "Prayer was always with a capital *P*. I felt like I should put on my Sunday clothes and wash my hands before I made the call to Mia." So he was praying with kid gloves, which took all the fun out of it. Once Mia broke the ice they began bringing their favorite readings into their Prayer Partner time: sometimes psalms and sometimes jokes. They also read parts of their journals to each other or shared something they'd learned that helped them stay strong. On a few occasions they watched an inspirational short on YouTube together. They brought everything they loved into their prayer time—which made them love their prayer time.

Mia and Neal aren't unique. When you pray the same way every day it is likely that your prayer life may get stale. That's as true for your prayer life as it is for your sex life.

Whatever makes us happy or brings us joy belongs in our prayer time; that goes for what makes us laugh or warms our heart or turns us on. What brings our prayers to life is the fullness of our feelings, and anything that engages our heart and soul is not only welcome, it's needed. Be creative.

The idea is not to do Prayer Partnering perfectly but passionately.

Praying together is the only part of Prayer Partnering that is not negotiable. Other than that, what you do together during those five to ten minutes can be of your own making. Use your imagination. Let your Prayer Partnering experience reflect who you and your Prayer Partner are.

I asked a dozen Prayer Partners what they have done to keep things fresh, and here is their list:

- Alicia includes music that she loves, some of which she writes herself. She finds that music helps her and her partner open their hearts. It makes their prayers more heart-centered.

- Doug and his partner do five minutes of journal writing during their prayer time: each writes out a devotional prayer and then reads it out loud. "It makes the time so spontaneous," he said, "and every day is new so we never know what to expect."

- Susan loves poetry more than anything in the world. She has taken it upon herself to bring a different poem to the prayer time each day. Jack *loves* that. He was never a poetry kind of guy, but Susan knows just the right poems that he might like. Susan says their prayers sound more like love poems to God.

- Nathaniel is a purist: "We sit in silence for a minute or two, and then we pray for ourselves and each other. Then we sit in silence for another minute together. And then if we want to, we share what's going on with us spiritually. If not, we're done. We don't deviate from that formula. I like knowing what to expect every morning, and so does Craig. We're both guys who don't like change much, so this works out great for us. Maybe I should start praying to be more flexible?!"

- Allie and her partner use art to connect creatively to the Divine. Both she and her partner color in a mandala each morning during the prayer time. "Granted," Allie said, "we spend way more than ten minutes, but we're both self-employed so we can get to work whenever we feel like it. Spending an hour with God in the morning is dreamy," she said. "We're floating by the time we hang up."

- Nikki confesses to doing the whole nine yards—incense, candles, singing bowl. "The works. I love the ritual of it all," she said. "I want to make my prayer space so beautiful so that God can't wait to come in." She said that setting the stage like this practically puts her in an altered state before she has begun praying. The vibe alone is enough to make her feel connected to her Holy Mother.

- Leslie and her Prayer Partner pray together for a minute or two only. Leslie says she doesn't feel a need to share more with her partner. "Having someone to pray with is the favorite part of my day. Those two minutes in the Kingdom of Heaven are pure bliss."

Ten Ways to Keep Your Prayer Partnering Fresh

1. Keep a journal.
2. Use background music.
3. Read a poem.
4. Choose a new place to pray.
5. Aromatherapy.
6. Candles.
7. New prayer.
8. Silence.
9. Sharing your spiritual successes.
10. Twittering.

Think about It

- *What elements would you like to include in your prayer time with your Prayer Partner? (For example, what might inspire your five senses?)*

Try This

During your prayer time experiment with different elements to feed your senses, to see if doing so enhances and deepens your prayer experience.

16.

Should I Keep a Journal During My Prayer Partner Experience?

Nancy got her best insights from writing in her journal. She said that she'd never kept a journal before, but after Prayer Partnering for a couple of weeks lots of coincidences started happening. There were too many to remember if she didn't write them down. "It was wild, one thing after another. People from my past called out of the blue . . . a neighbor put the right book in my hand when I most needed it . . . my boss moved me to a different department, which turned out to be perfect for me creatively." She said she'd never had so many interesting things happen in such a short period of time, and that praying with her partner was spiritually moving her life at warp speed.

The journal turned out to be a record of the way God was actively helping her in big and small ways every day.

She said that there wasn't even one day that God didn't give her some little things she needed. "I've always heard that life conspires to help you, but my journal was proof of it. There are hard days when my faith gets shaky, but I'd pick up my journal and read a page of the cool things that had happened and then poof! No more doubts. You can't argue with success, and that's what my journal has turned out to be—a success journal."

Brandon was a guy who couldn't see himself carrying around some girlie journal. He was particularly sensitive about artsy things like that, yet even he had to admit that writing in a journal bailed him out of some pretty "stinking thinking" on more than one occasion. "I'm in AA and when my head is screwed on backward some mornings, I'm a mess for the rest of the day. So my Prayer Partner suggested that we start our prayer time by listing ten things we're grateful for. See, I'm not writing, I'm listing. I know it sounds stupid, but then again I'm a work in progress. I'm only two years sober." Listing the things that are good in his life gets him back on track. Add prayer to that, he said, and he's ready to face the world again "without ripping some poor soul's head off at work."

Pat's a mom, four kids and counting. "I'm outnumbered!" she joked. "But I love every minute of the madness. My journal's my desert island—it's a time to hear myself think. Before I call Max to pray I take fifteen minutes to check in, and then we pray together. The next thing you know I feel ready to face my brood. It gives me a blast of energy that I'm going to need to get me through the day. Feeding my soul helps feed my body. How great is that?"

Peggy's journal has turned into a prayer book: pictures, poems, prayers, inspirational quotes she has collected, and lots of inspiring pictures she has cut out of magazines. Because it's small enough to fit in the back pocket of her jeans, she takes it with her wherever she goes. "When I'm stuck in line I pull it out and have a mini–Prayer Partner session with my journal," she said. All she has to do is open the journal to any page and within seconds she's smiling. She calls it her instant God fix.

There have been many studies over the last forty years about the healing power of keeping a journal. A study was done on a group of middle-aged businessmen who were unexpectedly terminated from their jobs. Over several months the group of men who had kept journals of their feelings about being fired and other life experiences found jobs twice as fast as the group of men who didn't express themselves in journals. In fact, at the end of the study the men who hadn't written in a journal were still unemployed.

Ten Things to Write about in Your Journal

1. Your successes
2. Gratitude list
3. Deeper questions
4. Your dreams
5. Your goals
6. Your struggles
7. Out-of-the-blue experiences, coincidences
8. Poetry
9. Favorite song lyrics
10. Inspirational quotes

Why Write in a Journal?

- To remind you of your successes
- To inspire you
- To uplift you
- To connect you to yourself
- To connect to Spirit
- To surprise you
- To remind you of what you're grateful for
- To record great inspirational quotes
- To write letters to Spirit
- To write your own psalms
- To record the ways that life has conspired to help you
- To record "out-of-the-blue" experiences
- To remind you of all the messengers life has sent to support you
- To list subtle answered prayers
- To discover that when things happened *to* you, they really happened *for* you
- To write what you learned each week that you didn't know
- To keep track of the way you're changing for the better
- To list the insights, epiphanies, and revelations that you've had

- To get clarity about any situation
- To move through obstacles more easily
- To clear the air: by writing letters you don't intend to send
- To get your secrets out of hiding
- To write down your wildest dreams
- To be honest about what you need
- To face your fear
- To write a love letter to yourself

Think about It

- *Have you ever kept a journal before?*
- *What was that experience like?*
- *What are your reservations about writing in a journal over the next ninety days?*

Try This

- If you've never written in a journal, go to a bookstore or office supply store and look at their selection of journals. See if any of them inspire you. If one does, buy it. You don't have to write in it now, but you might feel compelled to during your 90-Day Prayer Partner Experience.

- If you already have a journal, take a moment to write about what this experience has been for you, how you are feeling about the potential of Prayer Partnering right now.

17.

What Is Holding the High Watch?

The Tao te Ching, the 3,500-year-old philosophy of life, says, "All Life is a movement to our wholeness." This means that everything that happens to us is in actuality Life beckoning us to expand into our fullest potential. Psychologists call it the "urge to wholeness." The Talmud says that an angel sits over every blade of grass whispering for it to "grow, grow." All of life conspires to help us express our greatest life.

The trouble is that with our human eyes we see the experiences of our life as coming not to help us but instead to harm us. With our human eyes life looks like it's happening to us.

Only with the eyes of our soul (some say the eyes of our heart) can we see the truth: that all of life is happening *for* us.

It is the difference between seeing part of the story of our life—the narrow human point of view—versus seeing the whole story of our life—our Soul's destiny being lived through our human experience.

Peter stressed this point often when I would ask him how to "hold the High Watch" during the day. "Do I think good thoughts? Do I wish you well? Do I ask God to protect you during the day?" I didn't have a clue. That's why he decided to forgo our ten-minute limit and tell me the story of the Two Stones . . .

How we view our life is how we do our life.

There was once a wise old rabbi who throughout his life carried two stones with him at all times. His students speculated about why their teacher did this, and one day after class they approached him.

"Why do you carry two stones with you, Rabbi?"

"To remind me that I am fully human," he replied simply. The rabbi pulled the first stone out of his left trouser pocket and placed it in the palm of his hand. "This stone," he said, extending his left hand, "stands for my spiritual self. It is eternal and limitless: full of grace; it is never apart from God for a single instant. It says, 'Because of me the Universe was created.'"

"This stone," the rabbi said, removing the stone from his right pocket and placing it in his upturned right palm, "stands for my human self. Made out of the clay of the earth, it is limited and full of imperfection. And because it believes it is separate from the Source of life it causes no end of commotion in my world. It says, 'I am the center of the Universe.'"

"But Rabbi, why not just carry the spiritual stone?"
"Because we are both human and Divine, and it is within our ability to hold both sides of our nature so that we can fulfill God's desire for us—to be fully human. We must respect both sides of our dual nature; listening to them both . . . even dancing with them both!"

Peter finished the story and stayed quiet so that the meaning could sink in.

"What's this have to do with holding the High Watch for us?"

"Sweetie," Peter said, "most of us only know ourselves as the human self, so we deal with life from that level only. Once you know that you are Divine as well, then you can use your wiser eyes to see the world, and set the greater power within you to work in the world."

"So I'm supposed to look at my life through Divine eyes? That sounds great, but how do I do that?"

"You ask the question, 'How is what's happening *to* me happening *for* me?' When you do that you activate your soul's eyes."

"I just have to ask that question?"

"That question opens the deeper door within you," he said, "the place that knows that all of life is conspiring to help you grow. When you ask 'Why did this happen to me?' you're looking at life through a knothole in a fence—you can't see the whole story of what's really happening. When you ask, 'How is this happening for me?' the fence comes down and you can see the whole story of how the challenge is actually serving to make you stronger. Got it?"

"No!"

"The High Watch is knowing that every experience is meant to further us in our Destiny. Got it?"

"No!"

"Good. Call me tomorrow at eight to pray." Click.

Holding the High Watch and Prayer Partnering, like having a relationship with God, are not concepts to be learned in a classroom or through a lecture; they are processes. And processes can only be experienced. We have to have the experience; nobody can teach us; we have to walk that road for ourselves.

You keep the High Watch in your day for yourself and your Prayer Partner by seeing every experience that happens to you both by asking the question "How is this happening *for* us?"

Inevitably, you will begin to internalize the deep spiritual truth that everything is happening for you, and instead of feeling victimized, you will be able to see the gift of growth in each experience.

Ten Things You Might Want to Let Go of

1. Resentments
2. Thinking small
3. Resisting change
4. Relationships that don't work
5. Procrastination
6. Bad habits
7. Old clothes
8. Books you don't read
9. Guilt
10. Self-criticism

Try This

- *Think of a situation from the last decade that, at the time, seemed painful and difficult. In hindsight, how did that situation help to grow you?*

- *Think of something that is happening in your life now. Take a moment and ask the following question: Why is this happening for me?*

- *During the rest of your day, see what insights might be revealed.*

18.

What Do I Do If I Don't Feel Willing to Pray?

Our spiritual journeys are personal, each one as individual as we are, yet there are common experiences that we will share on our journeys. Obstacles aren't unique to us because, after all, we are the same family of man, human beings, one and all—there's no escaping that. "Human" might be the first name that sets us apart from other creatures, but "being" is our family name that we all share.

Chief Seattle put it another way: "Humankind has not woven the web of life. We are but one thread in it. Whatever we do to the web, we do to ourselves. All things are bound together. All things connect."

Sooner or later we will bump into our unwillingness— to get out of bed and pray, or to let go of what we've outgrown, or even to open and receive the answer to our prayer.

I'd been praying with Peter every morning at eight for over a month when one morning I made the call and it was clear that I was neither open nor willing. Peter could feel it and he called me on it.

"You're right, I'm not willing," I said. Where did this come from? For the last month I'd made remarkable strides. I felt as if I could see the light for the first time, breathe, be free to move forward instead of being stuck in the memory of an old relationship. "I'm mad that I'm doing all this work with you and Josh is probably off swindling the next girl out of her inheritance," I snorted. I didn't know where this unleashed anger came from, and frankly I didn't care.

Peter didn't say a word.

"You there?" I joked.

"I am, are you?"

"I am," I shot back, "right here."

"Your body's here, but not your heart. You're not here to pray, you're here to blame."

I knew he was right because the lightness I'd felt was gone. It had been replaced by the old tightness in my chest, the mean-spirited judgments floating through my mind. It felt like I had taken ten steps backward in my progress.

"When you're willing, give me a call and we'll pray together," he offered.

"I was willing before," I said, "but maybe you're right. Maybe I'm not anymore." How do you have it one day and lose it the next? I wondered.

"You were willing when you bottomed out with all that blame. But now that the pain is easing up a bit because the prayer's working, you're letting blame seep back in. You have to be even more vigilant now than you were before."

"What should I do?" I asked.

"Pray for the willingness."

"How do you pray for willingness when you don't feel willing?"

"You pray to be willing to be willing."

I was kinda, sorta willing but not entirely.

That whole day and night I put aside the Prayer for Forgiveness and prayed for one thing only: willingness. I knew that without willingness nothing was going to change for me. Without willingness I was still going to hate Josh forever and hate myself for not forgiving him. I expected this to be the hardest work I'd ever done. I braced myself for the uphill battle.

By the next morning something within me had shifted. While I was sleeping, the prayer, like a lantern in my hand, had led my feet to the path of willingness. I had a sense of commitment that I'd never felt before, a commitment that would see me through in my weak moments when blame begged me to open the door of my heart and let it in. Peter was right: when I was in pain it was easier to pray to ease the pain, but when

Ten Positive Affirmations

1. *I am One with Life.*

2. *I love Life, and all of Life loves me.*

3. *I embrace and accept all the good of God.*

4. *There are no obstacles in my life.*

5. *Thank you, God, for everything—I have no complaints whatsoever.*

6. *I am healthy and strong.*

7. *Every day, in every way, I am getting better and better.*

8. *I have all the love I desire.*

9. *The power of the Universe is my power now.*

10. *I am open to receive all of Life's riches.*

the pain was eased it was easy to forget and slip back into my old ways. Blame was my old friend. And while blame might intend to bury me alive, it came bearing gifts, even if the gifts were poisoned apples; in my mind they were still gifts.

The prayer "to be willing to be willing" worked in one day. The power of Prayer Partnering was blowing my mind. Never before had my prayers been answered with such speed, but then again never before had I prayed with such focus and depth and single-mindedness. Prayer Partnering had made me take praying very seriously; before, prayer was something I did only when I was in crisis, but now it was at the top of my list of things to do every day.

Think about It

- Where in this Prayer Partner experience are you unwilling?

- Is there any part of it that you are unwilling to commit to (e.g., being on time for the call, being prepared for the call, memorizing my prayer, etc.)?

- Are you willing to pray the prayer for willingness?

Try This

If you are truly willing to be willing, pray this prayer aloud a hundred times in the morning and the evening for seven days:

I am willing to be willing.

What Do I Do If I Don't Feel Willing to Pray?

19.

What Stands in the Way of My Prayer Being Answered?

This is the most important thing you need to know about your prayer being answered:

The way prayer works is that you either get the answer to your prayer or you get what stands in the way.

Most people do not know this about prayer, so when they pray and something unlike what they prayed for comes, they assume that:

- their prayer wasn't and won't be answered,
- God wasn't listening,
- they don't deserve the answer, or
- they prayed wrong.

We haven't been taught that everything that happens to us after we've prayed is a tiny piece of the puzzle to the answered prayer. Everything. So when you pray for peace and unexpected anger comes up in you, or you pray for love and you start to spew some old hatred that you thought was healed, even those things are to be considered part of the answer to your prayer. How else can you get to the peace or the love or whatever you want if what stands in its way isn't removed?

The Tao te Ching teaches that when you want something to shrink you must let it first expand. Eastern teachings insist that the obstacles that stand in the way to answered prayer can always be found within ourselves. That means that if there is something within blocking us, it has to come out of hiding.

Janice is someone who understood what stood in the way of her prayer being answered. She didn't fight it—she welcomed it as an answer to a prayer she did not know she had: to love herself. "Loving myself was the first step to being able to receive love from others."

Janice said that she received a big surprise from Prayer Partnering that had nothing to do with what she had prayed for. She prayed for a man to love her truly. She'd had plenty of affairs with men when she was a younger woman—she wasn't ashamed of that. But now that she was in her thirties she was ready for something more serious, and that's why she entered into Prayer Partnering, to find a man to love, and one who would love her. Oddly enough, she explained, she didn't get any man at all, not even one to pass the time with in a casual affair. Before, she had many men to choose from, but since she had begun praying with her partner, her phone didn't ring at all.

She started to wonder . . . was she being punished for praying for such a silly thing as someone to love, in the face of real problems like war and world hunger?

Then one night it hit her that she had never been alone in her life. She'd left her father's home and gone from man to man ever since. She had no idea what being alone with herself meant. What was harder for her to admit was that she didn't want to be alone with herself because she didn't like herself, let alone love herself. As a little girl maybe she had loved herself—she didn't remember—but not as a grown woman: there were too many things wrong with her to love. She'd made sure her calendar was booked with other people to ensure she didn't have to spend any face time with herself.

And here she was praying for true love when she didn't even love herself!

She made a commitment to her Prayer Partner right then and there: "I'm not going to date anybody for the ninety days that we're praying together." Instead, she said, she was going to date herself . . . finally.

This answer to her prayer felt so right that if true love didn't come, she didn't care anymore. Being able to love herself felt like the answer to an older prayer, one that her soul had been waiting for all her life. To love herself as she wished to be loved felt like the most perfect prayer in the world.

Thirty days into praying with her Prayer Partner, she made a decision to pray for self-love. She e-mailed me with this news. For the first time in her life, she said, referring to the Derek Walcott poem "Love After Love," she was in love again with the stranger who was herself. That was to change everything in her love life in the years to come.

Your prayer is answered every step of the way to "the answer." Janice's story is testimony to that, and so is Sonia's . . .

Sonia had been Prayer Partnering for seven months.

The last thing you should do is give up when your prayer hasn't been answered the way you imagined it would.

Her prayer was specific: "I want a husband." She was a lovely young woman who had come to my office to yell at me about how Prayer Partnering had brought her the exact opposite of the answer she had wanted. Instead of life bringing her a husband, her ex-husband had been sort of stalking her for the past six months. Every morning at five a.m. he would call, begging her to return to him and promising to change. By the time Sonia arrived at her office to begin her twelve-hour day as an orthopedic specialist, she was a mess.

"The calls are ruining my life," she told me.

I asked her if she wanted the calls to stop.

"After a three-year relationship, I left him last year. I left him." She over-enunciated. "Why on earth would I want him to keep calling? Especially since I had started praying with my Prayer Partner the month before the calls started . . . praying for a husband!"

Spiritual truth shows us that the more deeply we look at the stories of our lives with the eyes of our soul, we will find a trace of our own (usually unconscious) fingerprints on every situation.

"I tell him to go to hell every time we talk. You don't call that letting go?" she asked, without bothering to mask her sarcasm.

Contrary to popular belief, we attract not what we want but what we are. Which means that if we are holding on to something in secret, like a mirror our outer world is going to reflect it back to us. Sonia's situation was confusing because on the surface, it looked like her ex-husband would not let go of her; but in truth, unconsciously, for some reason, she must have been holding on to him.

She wouldn't hear of it. "I can't sleep knowing he's going to call me tomorrow. I hate it!"

The hallmark of blame is that it uses all our good energy, taking us in circles, never allowing us to drop down beneath the surface story of what is happening *to* us so that we can see the deeper story of why it is happening *for* us. The freedom we seek can be found only when we see the "whole" story, both sides, the place where *our* fingerprints play a part in the way things turned out. To our human mind and human eyes, only a fool would think that something seemingly "bad" could be happening *for* us. But the soul knows that all of life is a movement toward our wholeness: everything is part of the greater story of expressing our destiny. I was afraid that Sonia would bite my head off if I started in with these teachings, so I kept them to myself and directed her inward.

I asked Sonia to take her mind off the problem and focus on her breath instead. The breath is designed to lead us down beneath the surface appearance of things.

Sonia turned her attention to breathing for a minute or two.

I told her to ask the following question quietly to her deeper self: "Why won't Roger let me go?" I told her to repeat whatever she heard in response to the question. Whatever. She sat in the silence for barely a moment when an unbelievable answer came from within her: "I am holding on to him—he is not holding on to me."

I could see Sonia's body brace against the news. I told her not to argue with what came up, just keep breathing, and watch what emerged. And, sure enough, she reported that a picture arose in her imagination: the art deco bureau in her bedroom that she had inherited from her grandmother.

I asked her to describe it and she did. It was a highly lacquered mahogany bureau with a peach-tinted oval mirror perched on top. Displayed by shape and size lay various multi-colored perfume bottles and her mother's antique silver-handled brush set.

This appeared to have nothing to do with her ex stalking her, however. I encouraged Sonia to follow where the still, small voice of her intuition led.

"It tells me to open the drawers and see what's inside," she said.

In her imagination she saw herself opening the flat top drawer first. She stared at the contents of it in silence for a good minute.

"It's his jewelry . . . it's all the jewelry he's given me." Her ex-husband was an older man, a very rich older man. There before her eyes was her bureau drawer filled with the jewelry he had lavished upon her.

She described the gold and platinum rings, the pinky rings, the diamond drop earrings, the pearl choker, the various Tiffany pins and the silver and turquoise bracelets too numerous to count. Here were her invisible fingerprints on the story of why her ex-husband wouldn't let her go. She hadn't wanted to let all that expensive jewelry go. What if she never met a man who was as rich or generous with her? What if she could never afford to buy herself such gifts? And if something ever went wrong in her life, couldn't she always pawn the jewelry for cash? Unknowingly, the fearful what-ifs had tied her to his gifts, which tied her to him. "My intuition is telling me that I have to let the jewelry go," she said. Slowly she opened her eyes. She wasn't angry anymore. "I get it," she said, suddenly in a hurry for the session to be over. "I totally get it!" In the office waiting room I heard her cancel her dinner plans with a colleague before practically racing out the door.

I heard the rest of the story when she saw me the following week. She told me she had gone straight home from my office to her co-op apartment and walked straight to the bedroom bureau, as if she were on a mission. She opened the top drawer and stared at its contents for a long time. It was exactly as it had appeared in her mind's eye.

She went to the pantry, retrieved a brown paper bag more suited to bagging a lunch than bagging gems, and returned to her bedroom. She emptied every last piece of jewelry her ex-husband had given her, walked down the hallway, and, without hesitation, dropped the bag into the garbage chute and slammed it shut.

Only then did the unexpected, long-overdue flood of grief rise up from within her—the tears she had not shed for the loss of this relationship, which had had so many beautiful moments; the tears she had not wept for the loss of this man whom she had once loved, who had been very kind to her. The relationship had ended a year prior, but only now was she grieving the loss of it. Only now was she letting him go, as well as all of the riches he had given to her, the riches that had attracted her to him in the first place . . . the riches that had tied her to him—until now.

> ### Ten People You Might Want to Forgive
>
> 1. Yourself
> 2. Mother
> 3. Father
> 4. Brother, sister
> 5. Children
> 6. Boss
> 7. Teachers
> 8. Exes
> 9. Government
> 10. God

First thing the next morning Sonia called me. She was breathless. "He didn't call me this morning!" There was no five a.m. call as there had been for the last six months. "I'm sure there won't be any more calls," she said confidently. "I've let him go, him and his stuff . . . and it was really cool stuff." We laughed together at the bold, crazy audacity of her throwing away all that expensive jewelry rather than selling it, but she was certain it had been the right move for her.

Sonia could not truly open to another man until she had let go of her ties to this one. We think walking out the door is sufficient, but we often carry the energy of that experience—our emotional baggage—with us.

There was no telephone call from Sonia's ex that morning or any morning thereafter. Less than two years later she was married to a wonderful man. Why couldn't the wonderful man have come in answer to her prayer in the first place, we ask? He couldn't come in because there was no room. The obstacle that stood in the way of Sonia's answered prayer, or ours, dwells within ourselves. It needs to be moved out of the way so that there will be room for our heart's desire to enter.

Everything that happens after you pray is a part of the answer to your prayer. It's a waste of time to fight with whatever happens or resist it or run away from it or stop praying altogether. If there is something there, we must need to deal with it in some way, or heal it, or release it, or let it go. Often it looks like old relationship issues with our families or friends, bosses or loved ones. Take the step to complete the unfinished business and you will be one step closer to being open to receive the answer to your prayer.

Think about It

What things are coming up in your Prayer Partner experience that you are being invited to look at and resolve (e.g., you secretly don't like your job, there is someone you haven't yet forgiven, you are afraid of being alone, etc.)?

Try This

- *Use your journal to take these very things out of hiding. Write about them daily. See what positive ideas come up on the journal pages about how you might heal these unresolved issues in your life (e.g., counseling, making amends, seeing a doctor, joining a 12-step group, spending time in nature, etc.).*

- *When the positive ideas emerge, follow their wisdom and do what they instruct you to do in a timely manner.*

20.

How to Transmute Negative Emotions

"What do I do when I feel negative?" This was precisely the question I had for Peter when we prayed together, and as it turns out everyone experiences some negativity at one time or another during their Prayer Partnering.

"Here I am praying every morning with you and all the while I'm having some funky feelings?"

"Like how funky?"

"Like angry and judgmental and jealous. Not exactly holy, prayerful feelings."

"Just because you pray doesn't mean you're suddenly supposed to be a saint. Think of 'holy' as 'whole-ly,' " he said, spelling out the word for me. " 'Whole' means 'complete,' all parts of you present in the moment, that's all."

"I thought being holy meant being good."

"Sweetie, being 'whole-ly' is about being real . . . being your real self in every moment."

That was not at all what I had been taught in Hebrew school. One of the rabbis had a book in which he wrote down the transgressions of the students. In fifth grade, transgressions meant talking out of turn, or asking to go to the bathroom during class instead of waiting until the break. He called the black marks on our records "nekudot." Nekudot are dots, and his black dots carried a ton of weight—we were scared of them. We imagined that was what God's book of transgressions looked like: it was filled with pages of black dots. Being my real self had always landed me in the Book of Nekudot.

"Real, huh?" I asked cautiously.

He could tell I wasn't convinced. So he told me a story. It wasn't lost on me that Jesus was a teacher who taught through stories . . .

> There was an angry and discontented man who left his small town to visit with a rabbi, who was supposedly the wisest in the land. He found him in a village far away from home. The rabbi brought him to his study and they both sat down amidst the piles of books. The man couldn't help it—he blurted out his troubles, how he was an unforgiving man, how when he thought of his enemies he wished them ill, how he could more quickly curse than bless, how he could not love those closest to him or receive their love. "I cannot go on living this way," the man said, "not only for my family, but for me. Rabbi, what am I to do?"

The rabbi remained in silent contemplation for many minutes. Then he said, "I have a special statement for you to speak each time anything happens in your life that sets you off: Say, 'Thank you, God, for everything. I have no complaints whatsoever.'"

This sage advice suited the man. He thanked the rabbi profusely and with a light heart made the long journey back to his small town.

The following year the same rabbi, wiser still by a year, opened his door to the same man, who by his appearance was still angry and discontented. The man barged in and once inside launched into his story about how he had done what the rabbi had suggested, but here he was a year later, still the same man full of envy and rage and evil thoughts. His family had noticed no difference in him. He noticed no difference in himself. "Your wise advice was not wise after all," he spat out sarcastically.

The rabbi motioned for the man to come into his study and take a seat. The rabbi sat down in the well-worn chair by the hearth and was silent for many minutes. "Ah, I have a special statement for you to speak each time anything happens in your life that sets you off: Say, 'Thank you, God, for everything. I have no complaints whatsoever.'"

The man smiled, as if a light had been turned on from within his very soul. He understood. He was to say these words not only when good things happened in his life, but when the difficult things happened, he was to meet them with these words of gratitude. Especially then. When he stood up he was, indeed, a taller man and a wiser one even. He thanked the rabbi and made his return journey to his hometown as a happy man and remained so for the rest of his life.

"This is what they call the attitude of gratitude?" I asked.

"That's the modern term for it," Peter said, "but the principle of thanking God for everything—every single thing— is an ancient principle of truth that changes every burden into a blessing."

Our ten minutes was up ten minutes ago.

More than once I wondered in all seriousness if Peter had been that wise rabbi in another life, that teacher who had lived in Europe hundreds of years ago dispensing truth through simple stories.

Thank you, God, for everything. I have no complaints whatsoever.

Ten Things You Might Want to Forgive Yourself for

1. Unrealized goals
2. Comparing yourself to others
3. Unkind actions
4. Self-criticism
5. Not being "good" enough
6. Not doing enough
7. Procrastinating
8. Addictions
9. Old habits
10. Judging self and others

Try This

- *Cut out the declaration below, and place it where you will see it first thing in the morning and last thing at night.*

- *Take every opportunity during your day—at home, at work, while traveling or playing—to use this statement. This attitude of gratefulness is a muscle that requires building. The more you use it, the more it becomes yours.*

THANK YOU, GOD,
for everything—
I HAVE
no complaints
WHATSOEVER.

21.

What Happens at the End of the 90 Days?

Prayer Partnering is a process, and processes don't have a start and stop date attached to them; they are more fluid than that. By your ninetieth day your exact prayer may have been answered. Or it may not have been.

If your prayer hasn't been answered it doesn't mean that it won't be. It means that your prayer hasn't been answered *yet*. A lot of Prayer Partners will commit to praying together for another three months to see what happens. Your prayer could be answered in the sixth month or the ninth month or two years later, but you need to know that every step in this process will lead you toward your prayer being answered.

When you are praying with a partner, no step is wasted.

"Keep praying," said Jack, a banker who has been Prayer Partnering for almost five years now. "It's like money in the bank compounding interest every day!" One of Jack's prayers wasn't answered for over two years. "It's not that my prayer wasn't answered exactly; it's that I had to learn how to be a better man before I was ready to have it answered. It took a couple of years to learn how to become a guy who wasn't jealous every time a man looked at my wife, how to become a guy who didn't fly off the handle when I didn't get my way. I'd have made a lousy father if my prayer for kids had been answered the day I asked. When the answer to my prayer kept showing me that I had to fix *me*, I figured I'd better get to work. Two years went by, and now my wife's pregnant."

Glenn's prayer, on the other hand, took merely a week to be answered. "I found love six days after beginning Prayer Partnering. I bet I set some kind of a record," Glenn said. He had known Jill since college but had never seen her as anything more than a friend. "One day I looked at her like I'd never seen her before." Glenn said his prayer was to "'see love all around me,' and that day I swear I was looking through God's eyes, not mine, because I could see that Jill was just the kind of woman I'd been dreaming of. Why hadn't I seen it before?"

I, personally, waited eighty-eight days to receive the answer to my prayer. I woke up on a Wednesday morning and the heavy place in my heart where I'd been carrying a black stone with Josh's name on it was gone. I couldn't believe it. It was gone just like that, and in its place wasn't happiness or even relief, but an openness, a spaciousness I hadn't experienced since Josh. And before Josh. I've heard about healings like this happening to other people, but such a thing had never happened to me. I never believed it could.

I used to be nervous about calling something a miracle—how pompous, I'd think—until I learned that a miracle can simply be a "shift in perception." If that's the case, I surely did experience a miracle—I have not only forgiven the man who betrayed me, I thank him. "When I and enemy exist together," the Tao te Ching explains, "there is no room left for my treasure." While Josh might have looked like a strange angel, with the eyes of my soul I could see he was, indeed, an angel who came bearing Life's gifts that I am still unwrapping: the gift of Prayer Partnering, which has changed my life; and the gift of finding my true love, which has changed everything.

Ten Ways to Indulge Yourself

1. A luxurious bath
2. A day off
3. A weekend getaway
4. A walk along the beach
5. A drive through the country
6. Buying yourself something frivolous
7. A massage
8. A gourmet meal
9. Going to the theater
10. A dinner party with your close friends

22.

Am I Ready to Begin?

These pages contain my personal experiences with Prayer Partners, and those of all the Prayer Partners I've worked with over the years. Each had different things to say about how the Prayer Partnering experience affected our lives for the better. In essence, praying with a partner multiplied the answers to our prayers in mysteriously wonderful ways.

When we prayed together we were somehow a greater opening than we would have been praying alone. That we did it together made it all the more empowering: we became spiritual witnesses for each other's successes and growth. We didn't have to face our obstacles alone because we had a partner who would pray with us and for us, a partner in Spirit who held the "High Watch." No one had ever devoted themselves to supporting me spiritually like my partner did. You will be humbled by how sacred this relationship will become; and you will be blown away by what you will receive in prayer, those things you asked for and those you didn't. We were.

At first I thought it was Peter who changed my life, but when I was older and wiser I realized that what changed my life was the act of partnering in prayer with Peter; "gathering two or more in My name" unleashed a living presence in my prayer life that empowered both me and my prayers. Since those ninety days I've never stopped praying with a partner, and I have received answers to prayers too numerous to name: an amazing marriage, deeply meaningful work, a beautiful home in nature, a strong body and an open mind, and a relationship with God that is founded upon a solid rock of faith. I've received answers to my prayers that have proven to be blessings despite the fact that many of them at first glance looked like hardships.

From the moment you release your prayer, everything that happens to you—experiences both dark and light, expected and unexpected—is a tiny answer to your prayer. Every answer is meant as a stepping-stone that will lead you into receiving the answer to your prayer by *becoming* the answer to your prayers.

May your every good and true prayer be answered beyond your wildest imagination.

AUGUST GOLD *AND* JOEL FOTINOS

PART TWO

The 90-Day Prayer
Partner Experience

My Prayer Partner Commitment

Write a clear, concise prayer that you intend to pray with your Prayer Partner for the next 90 days.

My name for God: _____

Where God dwells: _____

What I am praying for (choose one thing):

_____

Write the prayer out as you will be speaking it (try to keep the prayer to twelve words or fewer):

_____

_____

_____

Signed Witness _____

Beginning of 90 Days (date): _____

End of 90 Days (date): _____

The 90-Day Prayer Partner Experience

Welcome to the 90-Day Prayer Partner Experience. We've designed 90 days' worth of brief devotions and meditations to help you and your Prayer Partner during the next three months. These devotions will help you to get the most out of your Prayer Partner experience; they consist of questions and information that will help deepen the journey. These daily guides also will serve to help you and your Prayer Partner stay on the same page—literally and figuratively. You may find that these 90 days of devotions will keep you focused on getting the most from this prayer time, and that they will also give you food for thought.

Your Prayer Partner experience is ultimately your own. What you bring to it you will get from it and more. The more committed you are, the more will come from it. This is true for any group or program you join (e.g., a recovery program, an exercise program, a retreat, etc.), and it is especially true for the 90-Day Prayer Partner Experience. Why? Because you have a partner to inspire and motivate you along the way. This is an exciting process, in which you choose to be each other's companions along the way.

Many of these devotions are about helping your Prayer Partner, many are about staying the course, many are about the benefits of Prayer Partnering and praying in general, and many others are inspiring words that we hope will lift you up. Do not be confined by these devotions. Add to them, change them, write in the margins, paste photos, and draw illustrations on the pages. In other words, think of the devotional section of this book as an interactive section, and literally make it your own.

How to Use It

This part of the book is designed to take you on a journey. Every day you will find a brief devotion that you can read to gain insight into the Prayer Partner experience, or ideas to inspire you and keep you motivated. Read them, meditate on them, ask yourself what part of the devotion speaks most to you, or what you would add to it. You might even read the devotion aloud with your Prayer Partner so that you both are bringing the words into your holy experience.

At the end of each devotion is a short, affirmative prayer. You can use this prayer with your Prayer Partner, taking turns saying it aloud to each other. You can also memorize this short prayer, so that you can recite it over and over to yourself all day long, which will help to make the prayer your reality for that day. Of course, if the prayer we've written doesn't speak to you, feel free to write your own affirmative prayer for each day as well.

You'll also notice that we've provided lines so you can record your thoughts for that day, and so that you can write down what you would like to choose for that day. This is a place where you can write down how your prayer experience went that day, or what you and your Prayer Partner are praying for, or any questions or struggles that come up, or questions you are asking of the Divine, or any other thing that is meaningful and helpful.

You can also use this space as a place where you can record your conscious choice of how you are going to live each day. We always have the power to choose our own experience, no matter what happens. When you state your intention for a day and then commit it in writing, you are using a powerful and time-honored tool to set your day on a certain course of your choosing. Yes, things will happen each day that you didn't predict, but when you begin the day with an intention, you are better equipped to handle all that happens to you. When you choose a positive intention for each day, you are more inclined to receive all the good that life has to offer you.

You can share these two types of journal entries with your Prayer Partner or not. You and your Prayer Partner can decide how best to use the written parts, and how they can add to your experience.

Ninety days is roughly thirteen weeks, so you will also find thirteen weekly exercises, which really are tips to help bring layers to your Prayer Partner experience. These exercises will add color and flavor and sound to your experience, and in turn will help you to maximize your prayer time. Do what feels right; don't do what doesn't. If one exercise doesn't resonate with you and your Prayer Partner, then take the opportunity to think of another one and do it instead. These exercises are not required; they are guidelines. These are tools and techniques that worked for us, and we hope they work for you as well. However, please shape the material in whatever way you need so that the 90-Day Prayer Partner Experience gives you what you need.

You'll also notice we often will use the word Life (with a capital *L*) throughout these devotions. When that word is capitalized, we are referring to that which is greater than ourselves. If you don't like that word, you can substitute a word you do like (e.g., God, Spirit, the Universe, etc.).

We hope you will not mistake what these devotions or written sections or exercises or even praying itself actually is about. These activities are not little games designed to keep you busy, and they are not magic acts that will bend Life to your demands. No, each of these activities is another way for you to connect to the Divine through your own soul. And by making that connection each and every day, you are putting yourself squarely in the flow of Life, which can then flow through you and take you on an incredible journey— your greatest life journey!

Week I Exercise

Select a special journal in which you can record your breakthroughs, "wins," and prayer manifestations. You can write down your thoughts, questions, struggles, and "aha" moments in your journal. The more you share of yourself in your journal, the more you will be able to hear what your soul is trying to tell you about the spiritual truth of who you are. Journals can serve as both a tool and a record of your Prayer Partner experience.

How much should you write in your journal each day? As much as your soul wishes to reveal through you. Some days you may end up writing half a page, while other days you may write three or four pages (or more). There is no hard-and-fast rule about quantity; what is most important is to use this tool consistently so that you can draw the most benefit from it.

You may want to choose a special journal—perhaps a leather-bound journal, or one that is otherwise specially bound—so that your Prayer Partner experience is given your deluxe attention. Or you may get a plain journal and decorate it with artwork (that you create, that you cut out of magazines or other sources) so that it feels very personal. Or you may want to choose a journal small enough to keep with you, in your pocket or your purse, so that you can use it all day long. Choose carefully so that you will use your journal every day.

Day 1 . . . Getting Started

Beginning is both the hardest thing to do and the most liberating thing we can do. By starting we are putting into motion a new path, a new journey, and a new life experience. Starting is a brave thing to do, a way of breaking out of the comfortable and known and moving forward in your own life so that every choice can create a new reality. Working with a Prayer Partner is one of the most powerful actions you can take to create this new reality. Working together will bring a greater experience and understanding for you both. Congratulations on beginning your journey.

Today I choose to begin anew, knowing that I can
choose anew every moment of the day.

Day 2 . . . Awkward

Working with a Prayer Partner can feel a bit awkward at the beginning. How do we pray? What will work? Do we have to pray aloud? All of the questions we have are present, and we can sometimes feel vulnerable and shy, especially if we are new to prayer. This is where working with a Prayer Partner can help. You are no longer alone on the spiritual journey. You have support, and a partner who is constantly seeing the greatest within you. For now, know that the initial feelings of awkwardness will fade as you pray together each day and get to know the rhythm of this prayer relationship. It's okay for it to feel unusual at first, because working with a Prayer Partner is not usual, it's extraordinary!

Today I allow myself to feel whatever I feel, and then
move forward anyway.

Day 3 . . . Finding Your Feet

When we are in the beginning of a journey, it can take us a few days (or more) to find our footing. That is true as well with Prayer Partnering; it can take a few days or so to find out what really works, what you like to do, what you don't like, what time works best, and so forth.

Give yourself the option of making adjustments, trying some new things, evolving your Prayer Partner experience so that it lifts you up. This is not just prayer that you are doing; this is invoking a new way of living and being in the world. You are literally relearning how to begin your day, which in turn will change the experience you will have each day.

Today I trust the journey that Life is taking me on.

Day 4 . . . What Inspires You?

One of the best ways to benefit from your Prayer Partner experience is to find something inspirational and bring that to the Prayer Partner daily meeting. For instance, you may find the lyrics of a certain hymn or song inspiring; you may want to use those words (or sing them) during your time with your partner. Inspirational literature and sacred works are wonderful places to find words to uplift and inspire you.

Poetry, prayers, quotes, sayings, even an inspirational section of a novel—anything that lifts you and your partner to the highest state of mind can be used in your morning experience. Be creative and have fun!

Today I find inspiration everywhere I look, and I in turn inspire others.

_____

_____

Day 5 . . . Guidance

A very powerful prayer to use when you don't know what to pray for is this: "I am open for guidance." To ask Life to guide us to our highest and greatest life experience is to open ourselves to follow where Life will take us. The Universe is a friendly place, and when we ask It to help us, It will. Part of our journey in these 90 days with our Prayer Partner is to learn to trust in Life, to trust ourselves, to trust our partner, and to trust that everything is conspiring to bring us to greater realizations and greater life experience.

Today I allow Life to guide me to my good.

_____

_____

Day 6 . . . Holding the High Watch

Having a Prayer Partner is a marvelous responsibility. In this relationship, one of our gifts is to "hold the High Watch" for our partner. What does that mean? Holding the High Watch means to see the greatest potential within our partner, to imagine that potential is realized, and that this realization has already happened for them. Holding the High Watch is a way of witnessing our partner, believing more for them than they often can for themselves. The wonderful part? As we do that for our Prayer Partner, they are doing it for us. It can become a deep and profound relationship, all based on Divine Love.

Today I hold the High Watch for my Prayer Partner.

Day 7. . . Commitment

There is power in making a decision and taking action. And there is even more power in staying committed to this positive action. Similar to working out in a gym, when we commit and follow through with our Prayer Partner, we are building spiritual muscle that strengthens us. Every day we can choose again to commit to our partner, commit to our own spiritual growth, and commit to Life. This is your moment now: choose once again to commit to Prayer Partnering and you'll find that the gift of this commitment returns to you tenfold.

Today my commitment to my own spiritual life increases and blesses me.

Week 2 Exercise

Life is always wanting to communicate with us. The more we listen, the more we will be able to hear what It is always trying to tell us. We can be creative in how we listen to Life. One way that can benefit your Prayer Partner experience is very simple but can be very profound.

Go to the inspirational section of your local library or bookstore, or even to the spiritual books on your own bookshelves, and pick a spiritual book at random. It could even be the Bible, the Tao te Ching, or another book of sacred writing, or a spiritual book that you've read before and loved, or one that you've always wanted to read but haven't gotten around to it yet, or even one you've never heard of before.

Whichever book you choose, hold it in your hands and close your eyes for a moment. Think about your Prayer Partner, the prayers you both have, and hold that thought for a moment. Then open the book at random and look at the pages you've opened to. Read them and see if anything jumps out at you, any piece of wisdom that seems to pertain to your and your partner's prayers. If nothing jumps out, open the book and try it again.

Day 8 . . . Soul Meeting

The Prayer Partner relationship is unique in that you become close with each other not through the "normal" ways of sharing (your past, your wounds, your daily lists or weekend plans, for instance), but through the meeting of your souls. Spending five or ten minutes daily coming together in prayer, whether in person or on the phone, creates a bond and a spiritual intimacy that runs far deeper than most "worldly" relationships. What's amazing is that since the soul knows no time or place, it doesn't matter if you meet on the phone or in person, because you both are connecting on the level of the soul.

Today my soul speaks to me and guides me every step of the way.

Day 9 . . . Continuing

Sometimes we reach a fork in the road of our life where we are asked to make a decision: continue on or take a different path. Our intuition will tell us the best way to move forward, which path to take. It is important to make that decision from a place of peace and balance, rather than from a place of fear or doubt or confusion, because often those emotions will cloud our choice. Sometimes the best choice to make is to continue on the path we are on. Our fears and doubts can tell us to bail out, to take what looks like an easier path—but our soul will always guide us to the path that is for our highest and greatest good. If you feel you are at a fork in the road of your life, take a breath, ask your Prayer Partner to hold the High Watch for you, and then take this decision into prayer.

*Today I rise above my fears and doubts and keep
moving forward in my life.*

Day 10 . . . Breaking through Resistance

Whenever we begin on a new spiritual journey, we go through several stages of emotions. Often the beginning is exciting, because we are doing something new and we have a clear outcome in mind. But just as often, once the excitement of the new activity fades, our resistance begins to come to the surface. Our resistance is a mechanism that we've installed in ourselves to protect us from real change. Resistance can be something that keeps us from reaching new levels in our life, because there is a part of us that doesn't want anything to change, that fears what would happen if we actually got what we wanted. If you feel resistance to Prayer Partnering, ask yourself, what am I really resisting? The Prayer Partner experience is bringing something important to the surface, and this is the opportunity to discover what it is so that you may go beyond it safely and with confidence.

Today I choose to listen to my inner voice, rather than my fears or resistance.

Day 11 . . . Rhythm of Life

A wonderful by-product of Prayer Partnering is that you begin to live in the rhythm of Life, rather than the frantic, chaotic rhythm of fear. When we get into the rhythm of Life we find that Life always moves at a certain pace; Life is not concerned with our pushing and shoving to make things faster or slower. Life moves as Life moves. And our prayer time is a way we can connect to that movement and begin to move in rhythm with Life, rather than try to fight or change it. There is a saying that goes "God is always right on time," and the Prayer Partner experience helps us to tell the time correctly!

Today I am in rhythm with the rhythm of Life.

Day 12 . . . Joy

What is your prayer? Whatever you are praying for, you might consider adding "joy" to it. Joy is an essential ingredient to living a life that is satisfying and purposeful. Without it, we're often told, life isn't worth living. How joyful are you? How much joy do you want? Or better yet, how much joy can you receive? Joy can heal us, motivate us, help us, comfort us, and take us on a journey unlike anything else. After a while, once we get a taste of true joy and how it fuses us with our soul's journey, we will discover something incredible: joy *is* the journey.

Today I receive and embrace joy in my life, and as my life.

Day 13 . . . Wonderfully Made

The sacred texts tell us something that we often forget: that each of us is wonderfully and lovingly made. Each of us is here for a purpose, for a reason. There are no mistakes in the Universe. Each day is another opportunity to realize this very profound truth, another opportunity to remember it more fully than the day before. Each time we pray with our partner we get to hear this truth in their voice, and we get to mirror back this truth to them. Your Prayer Partner can remind you, when you can't remember it for yourself, that you are already wonderfully made.

Now it's time to live as if you know it!

Today I remember that I am wonderfully and lovingly created.

Day 14 . . . One Deep Well

There is an old saying on the spiritual path that it is better to dig one deep well rather than twelve shallow ones. What this means is that we can often be scattered and dissipate our energies, and when we do this it yields very little in our life, if anything at all. But when we stay focused on one thing, we can receive much from it—more understanding, more blessings, more gifts, more experiences. When we are not clear about who we are and what we want, our life seems to mirror that lack of clarity and in turn gives us nothing specific. Conversely, the more clear we are, the more our life will in turn reflect that as well. Your Prayer Partner experience will help you to stay focused and dig one amazing deep well within yourself, and keep you from scattering your gifts away.

Today I stay focused on who I am and what I want.

Week 3 Exercise

It is important to pay attention during these 90 days to all the ways that your prayers will be answered. Many times our prayer is answered, but not necessarily in the way we thought it would be, and our Prayer Partner can be helpful in identifying how our prayer is being answered when we sometimes can't see what is happening because we are too close to it. The reason it is important to pay attention and see how our prayer is answered is so that we can see how Life is always working to make our intentions come to fruition. Our prayer takes on new confidence the more we see that it is being answered.

Begin keeping a list—perhaps call it "Answered Prayers," or something like this. You can keep this list either in your journal or on a separate piece of paper, but wherever you keep it, keep it close by so that you look at it daily. Looking at this list will remind you of answered prayers, and it will also keep you focused on expecting answers to your prayers. That expectation helps to create your openness for an answer to come!

Share your list from time to time with your Prayer Partner, and ask your partner to do the same with theirs. By sharing these answers you can also help each other see even more ways that the prayers are being answered. The more open you are, the more ways, no doubt, you will see that Life conspires to bring your heart's desires right to you.

Day 15 . . . Living Waters

Does your life ever feel parched? Dry? Empty? Have you had times when your life feels so hot, like an intense desert? Everyone goes through these periods when life gets hard and inspiration is hard to find. This is when a Prayer Partner can be especially helpful, for they can act like a lighthouse, always pointing you back within yourself, which is where you will find the stream of living waters that will quench all that is parched. Within you are the living waters that are the Source of Life itself. Within you is where you will always find it, and your Prayer Partner can gently remind you of this truth. And, in turn, you will no doubt have the opportunity to remind your Prayer Partner of this same truth.

*Today I go within and experience the living waters of
my soul.*

Day 16 . . . Keep It Private

One way that the ancient mystics used to maximize the
spiritual power they were discovering within them was to
keep it private. They didn't share their spiritual process with
anyone and everyone; instead they chose to share their experiences only with those who could truly understand. In so
doing they contained the energy of the spiritual discoveries,
keeping them holy. The Prayer Partner Experience can act in
the same way. What you and your partner share with each
other within the daily Prayer Partner meeting should remain
private between the two of you. Not only does that honor
the important pledge of confidentiality, but it also will keep
the spiritual truths you experience from being diluted.

*Today I hold my prayers and those of my Prayer Partner close
in my heart, knowing they are manifesting now for us both.*

Day 17. . . First Resource

I have a small sign in my office that says prayer should be your first resource, not your last resort. Often we will try every other method we can think of to help ourselves when life gets difficult, and then we only turn to prayer as a last, desperate act, almost like a losing football team's Hail Mary pass. Since life always mirrors back what we believe, when we pray desperate prayers, we often get desperate results. But when we begin with prayer, we are approaching our lives and every situation in it from the highest emotional, mental, and spiritual place possible. The result? Life will mirror this as well, and we will be living our lives proactively with prayer rather than desperation.

Today I begin with prayer and I allow my prayer to guide my day.

Day 18 . . . Spiritual Love

There are many different kinds of love—love of a parent for a child, love between committed adults, love for a nation, love of a book, and so forth—but there is one form of love that the ancient Greeks called the "highest" form of love, and that is love called agape, which is translated as "unconditional love." This is spiritual love, and this love comes from the soul. We all have access to this agape love, and every day that you pray with your Prayer Partner you are accessing that spiritual love within yourself and sharing it with your partner.

Today I give and receive unconditional love.

Day 19 . . . Breathe

Have you ever stopped to think about how sacred our breath is? The very breath we breathe is a gift we have, and it is available to us all the time, effortlessly. This is true of our inner wisdom as well; it is as available to us as our breath. In fact, when we breathe deeply, we can calm ourselves and allow ourselves to go to that inner, unlimited source of wisdom within. The more deeply we allow ourselves to breathe, the more deeply we can connect to our Source. You may want to begin each prayer session—with your partner, and when you pray by yourself—with a few deep breaths, so that you are touching the Inner Voice within. When you do, that Inner Voice will breathe through you, and you through It.

Today I breathe in Life deeply, and I exhale Life deeply.

Day 20 . . . The Law of Exponentiality

In junior high math class we learned about the concept of exponential numbers. This is when a number is multiplied by itself, rather than added to itself; 8 × 8 will give you a much bigger result than 8 + 8 will. This is how Prayer Partnering works. The result of praying with a partner will be exponentially larger than when you pray by yourself. There is no scientific explanation for this, but there is a spiritual explanation. I call this the Law of Exponentiality. It's as if adding another person who is an active witness and supporter of your prayer can often exponentially increase the power of the prayer—both your prayer and the prayer of your partner. Every morning that you pray with your partner, you are practicing the Law of Exponentiality in your lives.

Today my prayer experience is expanded by the power
of praying with my Prayer Partner. All is well.

Day 21 . . . Stay Inspired

Some days the inspiration just seems to flow easily and effortlessly. And then some days it seems like the reverse is true—that inspiration is harder to come by. When we have one of those days when it feels like Life is being stingy with inspiration, we can turn things around by doing what is called "overcompensation." To reverse the flow when it feels as if our spiritual progress is on the decrease, we simply need to increase our devotional time. Recommit to everything that inspires you, including your Prayer Partnering, read inspirational literature, listen to inspirational music—literally flood your life with positivity. When inspiration is hard to come by, we have a choice. Either we can live the day uninspired, or we can engage in the very practice that will change the direction and open up the flow again.

Today I flood my life with positive thoughts, words,
and actions.

Week 4 Exercise

Keeping your Prayer Partner experience fresh is important. It's best if the time you spend with your partner doesn't feel like a duty or something you dread. There are times when this will happen, and often it is because of the resistance or fear that we may experience, and this is normal during the Prayer Partner experience. Sometimes we can get into a rut with our prayer time, and it is good to try some variations so that we can stay focused, excited, and motivated to keep our 90-day commitment (and even beyond that).

One way that you can add some depth and color to your Prayer Partner experience is to add music to your prayer time. Music is a language that our soul understands and responds to. We've probably all had the experience of hearing a song that we haven't heard in a long time, and by hearing that song we are reminded of an experience or time in our lives. Why? Because our soul remembers music and listens to what it says. By adding music to your prayer time, you can add something that will enhance your experience by involving another soul sense.

The kind of music you add is important. Obviously, loud hard rock or rap music are probably not the most productive choices. Music is meant to enhance, not dominate, your prayer time. Choose music that lifts you up, inspires you, elevates your experience. Classical music can be good, as can "New Age" music. Instrumental music works best, in general, though some vocal music can work as well, such as Gregorian chant or Celtic music.

You can use the music as background, or if there is a particularly inspiring song that you want to play during your short Prayer Partner time, that could be a way to add to your prayers. Music should never take the place of your prayers, but when used correctly music can make your Prayer Partner experience more potent.

Day 22 . . . Be the Message

There are three levels of truth. The first is to know a truth, which is the level where we understand the concept in our head and we know that it is true. The second level is to practice that truth, which is what we do as we try to live that truth in our lives. And the deepest level is to "be" the truth. This happens when you no longer need to even think or practice the truth, because that truth is within you and you are one with it. This can be a truth such as peace, or love, or generosity, or forgiveness. Working with your Prayer Partner is an excellent way to move from a level of knowing something, to living it, to being it.

Today my life is in alignment with my beliefs and my dreams.

Day 23 . . . A Grateful Life

A mystic once wrote that "Life rewards a grateful heart," and when I read that, it inspired me to write in my journal, "A grateful heart will create a great-filled life." The most powerful way to go through a day is to do so in a state of praise and thanksgiving. To give praise for your life, no matter what it looks like, is the single most powerful spiritual tool you can use to live fully and freely in your life. When we give thanks—whether life is good and even when life doesn't seem so good—we are invoking the spiritual Law of Thanksgiving, which states that when you are grateful, you are open to receive more to be grateful for. Jesus stated it this way: to him who has, more shall be given, to him who has not, all shall be taken away. Life always mirrors our thoughts and intentions. Your Prayer Partnership is an excellent way to stay in a state of gratitude and cultivate a grateful heart.

Today my grateful heart creates a great-filled life.

Day 24 . . . Taking Your Life Seriously

"Take me seriously," we sometimes will say to someone else, when we feel they are not paying us close enough attention. But I've noticed that the one person who often takes us the least seriously is ourselves. We say that we are going to do something, and then don't follow through. We say that we believe something, and then we act in an exact opposite way. We berate ourselves for not looking a certain way, or we can't forgive ourselves for something we've done. We often treat ourselves in ways that we wouldn't treat even a casual acquaintance. By committing to our Prayer Partner experience, we are choosing to do something amazing: we are taking ourselves seriously. And the more seriously you take this experience, the more you will be taking your life seriously, and the more Life will take you seriously.

Today I live as if I mattered. I am here for a reason.

Day 25 . . . Asking for Help

Sometimes we feel we have to do everything by ourselves. Do you ever feel as if it is easier to just do something yourself, because it will be faster and done the way you like it? That may work well for your job or other areas, but that attitude does not always help you on the spiritual path. While it is true that we ultimately are 100 percent responsible for our own lives, we can do something that is radical for many people: we can ask for help. Whom should you ask? Two answers come to mind. First, you can ask your Prayer Partner to help by praying for something specific for you, and knowing with you that the answer is on the way. Second, you can ask Life itself to help you. Life will require you to give up total control over whatever it is you are asking help for before It can help—because Life can only do for you what it can do through you. Ask for help, and then let go and let Life.

Today I ask for the help I need, and I accept the help
I need.

Day 26 . . . Honey in the Jar

A teacher once told me that when we pray for someone else, we also get some of what we are praying for them. For instance, if we are praying for prosperity for someone else, we will also receive prosperity ourselves. "It's like honey in a jar," she said. "When you pray for someone else, you are the jar and the honey is the blessing flowing through you. And like honey, some of it will stick to you. This works both ways, of course," she added. "When we wish ill in any way for someone else, that sticks to us as well." Every time you pray for something for your partner, you are in essence also opening to receive that blessing for yourself.

Today I pour forth blessings, good thoughts, and positive expectations for others, and know that I experience these things for myself as well.

Day 27. . . Dark Nights

A dark night of the soul is when we feel abandoned by Life, and all that Life has to offer us. One of the main traits of a dark night of the soul is feeling alone or even abandoned. Having a Prayer Partner is a way through the dark night, a way to go through it with spiritual support. My friend may say that a Prayer Partner has "got your back," meaning that they will look out for you, and help in the ways they can. And you get the privilege of doing the same for them when they need it. With your Prayer Partner and with Spirit, you are not alone.

Today I know that I do not walk alone.

Day 28 . . . Peace

A teacher I once sat down with said that peace is not something you get; it's something you practice. "There is an art to practicing peace," the spiritual teacher said, "and that art is to see peace in everything, especially in the things that look anything but!" What he meant is that peace already exists and is underneath everything that exists. If we can look at what does not seem peaceful and see through that veneer to the peace that exists within it, we are in essence seeing through what is the lesser and into the greater. This may sound like a paradox, and we cannot do this on the merely human level. We need to look at every situation through a spiritual lens, and that lens is a benefit we gain from our Prayer Partner experience. Each day that we pray with our partner, we are learning to see the truth in everything, including that which seems like the opposite.

Today peace is my compass, and it leads to where I can experience and give peace.

Week 5 Exercise

Since you and your Prayer Partner are meeting on the level of the soul each morning, you are creating a strong bond that runs deep. Doing your daily prayers together is changing your life in a profound way. In addition to the short, daily call, it is important to check in with your Prayer Partner regularly to make sure that you both are having the optimum experience, and to see if there are more ways you can support each other as Prayer Partners.

If you and your Prayer Partner live in the same city or area, make a date to meet to talk about your Prayer Partner experience. Meet in person if possible, although meeting on the phone is fine as well. You will need an hour or more, so find a place where it will be easy to talk, where you won't be interrupted often, and where you can concentrate on your partner and this discussion.

You can discuss what to keep in your prayer routine, what to change, and what breakthroughs, "wins," and manifestations you have had and those you have observed in your partner. This can be a time to help each other to see your lives in the context of prayer, how prayer is changing you, even where you can't see it for yourselves. By discussing your thoughts, experiences, struggles, and wins, you are sharing from the deepest level, soul to soul. This is not a time of therapy or talking about what you did over the weekend. Our Prayer Partner is not our therapist, and our Prayer Partner time is not to be used to discuss the mundane. Use this time with your Prayer Partner to stay focused on your spiritual process, and that of your partner. Ask each other leading questions, such as "What do you like most about the Prayer Partner experience?" or "In what surprising ways is Life answering your prayers?" When you ask each other questions, you are opening up the conversation to share at the soul level.

By doing this, you are in turn creating an even deeper Prayer Partner experience.

Day 29 . . . Starting Your Day

Years ago I would begin each day by turning on the television and listening to the news of the morning. Who killed whom, where war was raging, what businesses were failing, what celebrity was acting erratically. Then I would read the newspaper and see again all of the so-called news of the day, which was similar to what was on television, but there was more of it. And then I would go to work depressed and have a lousy day. It took me a long time to connect that how we begin each day will largely determine what kind of day we are going to have. Starting each day with our Prayer Partner, in daily prayer, allows us to begin each day with spiritual truth, and puts everything else in context. Then, when we are confronted with the news of the world, we can use our spiritual insight to help bring peace to a world that sometimes looks anything but peaceful. Starting your day in prayer is good medicine for you, and for the world around you.

Today I start my day consciously and connect deeply
with the Divine.

Day 30 . . . Pray All Day

One question people often ask about Prayer Partnering is "What do I do the rest of the day?" They want to know how to continue their morning prayer experience through the rest of the day. The answer, of course, is to pray all day. On the surface this seems like a difficult thing to do, maybe even impossible. But prayer is more than just words spoken; prayer is also an attitude, a way of being. We can carry that prayerful attitude with us all day long. It may take some time and practice to build up to this, but what a gift once we do. We will be living each day in a place of high spiritual energy—and in turn we will begin to see that each day is holy.

Today is a day of prayer in action. My prayer is my way of walking in this world.

Day 31 . . . No Limits

How much good can you accept? How much joy are you willing to have? How much healing or love or peace do you want? There are no limits in the Universe, yet many of us walk around as if we are paupers in mind, body, and spirit. We place so many limits on ourselves, either by choice, or by believing that these limits are fixed in stone. What the mind can conceive, we're told, the mind can achieve. Where do we go to turn our dreams into reality? Bring them to your Prayer Partner experience, turn them over to Life, and know that they are on their way.

Today I accept no limits in my life, or in anything that happens to me.

Day 32 . . . No Emergencies

A best-selling author once told me, "For a while it seemed as if every emergency came forth in my life, one after another." What did you do? I asked her. She explained that she examined the root cause of the emergencies. "I saw how I was feeding off those emergencies, how they were fueling something in me, and how those emergencies were keeping me from doing what I wanted to do by keeping me doing what I have to do." After she had that profound revelation, she and her Prayer Partner decided to say a special prayer each morning: "There are no emergencies. I do not create emergencies, and I do not adopt the emergencies of other people." After a while, she said, the emergencies stopped, in part because she didn't give them any energy to keep coming. Praying every day with her partner helped her to move beyond the level of emergencies and drama, to one of creative openness.

Today I do not create any emergencies, and I do not adopt the emergencies of others.

Day 33 . . . Forgiving

Forgiveness is a potent spiritual medicine that can literally change your life in an instant. The key to forgiveness is willingness, and if willingness is hard to find, you can always pray to be willing to be willing! If you look at the Prayer for Forgiveness, you can see that there are three parts to forgiveness. The first part is forgiving others who have harmed us. It is through prayer that we are able to bring our awareness to the power of forgiveness when someone has caused us damage or harm in some way. Your refusal to forgive another does not hurt them, but it is lethal for you. On the other hand, your willingness to forgive another at the right time sets you both free, and breaks the prison that blame creates. Make a list of those whom you need to forgive, and bring that list into your Prayer Partner experience. Pray to be willing, or at the very least, to be willing to be willing. And let Life—and your Prayer Partner—help you.

Today I am willing to forgive (or willing to be willing to forgive) those who have harmed me.

Day 34 . . . This Is the Day

One of my favorite verses in the Bible is, "This is the day the Lord has made; we will rejoice and be glad in it" (Psalms 118:24). More than a nice slogan, this verse actually holds a powerful spiritual lesson that we can use when praying with our partner, and beyond. What this verse is asking us to do is to remember each and every morning that the only day we are given is today. When we know this deep in our being, rather than just as a sweet concept, then it becomes a great motivator to live each and every day to the fullest. And the greatest attitude we can have in each day is one of rejoicing. Each morning as you pray with your partner, pause for a moment to remember that this is truly the day that has been given to you—the only day you can live—and it is right and good to give thanks for it.

Today I know that this is the day that the Lord has
made, and I rejoice and am thankful in it.

Day 35 . . . There Are No Obstacles Here

A Course in Miracles states that there is a powerful prayer
that can be said when you find yourself in the midst of a
difficult situation and you feel that there is no solution in
sight. Pray, with all of your heart and mind and soul, these
words: "There are no obstacles here." Know it and believe
it. The level of mind that created a situation can never be
the same level that will find the solution. By declaring that
any and all obstacles are now gone, what you are doing is
lifting yourself out of the lower level of the problem into
the higher level of the solution. Know this for yourself, and
know it for your partner as well.

Today I know that there are no obstacles to my good.

Week 6 Exercise

The Prayer Partner experience can serve as a way to find our center and our balance, and help us to then live from that centered and balanced place. One way we can accentuate this for ourselves, which in turn will accentuate the experience for our partner as well, is to spend a few moments before our daily prayer session with our partner in silent meditation. This period of time can open you so that you are ready to receive all that your Prayer Partner experience will be for that day.

If possible, try to spend the five (or even ten) minutes before your Prayer Partner call meditating. If you already have a meditative practice, you can do that. If you do not already have a meditative practice, try closing your eyes and focusing on your breath for those five or so minutes. If it is hard to just focus on the breath, try this method: with each breath in, think the words "Life is . . . ," and then with each breath out, think the words "I am . . ." If those words don't resonate with you, substitute words that do.

You can also spend those few minutes before the call reading inspirational literature or listening to inspirational songs (see the list of "Ten Songs to Inspire You" on page 33). Pick a book like the Tao te Ching, or the Psalms, or a book by a spiritual master such as Ernest Holmes or Joel Goldsmith, and allow the words to lift you, so that when you call your partner you are already operating from a very high altitude. See how doing this will bring a new awareness to your Prayer Partner experience.

Finally, if you really want to take your Prayer Partner experience further, also spend the five to ten minutes after your Prayer

Partner call in meditation, listening for the voice of Life gently guiding you and loving you. Life always has something to say to us, and is always lifting us up and moving us forward. What an amazing way to begin each and every day!

Day 36 . . . Batteries

My son brought his battery-operated toy train to me and said it was going slow and labored. "Probably the batteries are low," I told him. The toy took two AA batteries to make it run, but I had only one new battery. I took out one of the old "low" batteries and replaced that one with the new "fresh" battery. The train instantly moved faster. The combined power of the old and new battery together was enough to get his train moving effortlessly again. It can be like this with our Prayer Partner. Sometimes we are like the old battery, running low on power. Our partner can be our fresh battery, causing both of our lives to run effortlessly again. And you can be a fresh battery for your partner as well. And allow Life to recharge your spiritual batteries as well.

Today I am recharged, and I allow my energy to flow forth freely.

Day 37 . . . Fear of Getting What We Want

One Prayer Partner I had kept praying for a particular outcome that never seemed to come. "Why doesn't this come to me?" he asked in frustration one time. "Maybe you are afraid it will come true, so your fear keeps it away," I replied, and then suggested that we bring his frustration into our prayer time, and he agreed. As his Prayer Partner, I thought that maybe his frustration was showing up in his life for a reason; perhaps it was trying to reveal to him something important. A few days later he excitedly told me that using our prayer time to deal with his frustration had worked wonders. He had a surprising revelation in which he was shown that he was afraid of actually getting his heart's desire. He had not expected this and did not know this fear was in his subconscious. Once it was revealed, we brought that fear into our prayer time, and sure enough, eventually his desired outcome manifested in his life.

*Today I fear nothing in my life, neither lack nor
limitation of any kind. I accept all the good that Life
has to offer.*

Day 38 . . . Consistency

One person asked me why the prayers she and her Prayer Partner were praying never seemed to be answered. I asked how often they prayed, and she told me that they didn't pray every day, usually only two or three times a week, unless one of them had a hectic week or was out of town. Immediately I could understand the problem: these partners weren't committed to a consistent prayer schedule; they were doing their Prayer Partnering in a halfhearted way. The recovery movement reminds us that halfhearted measures will avail nothing, and I believe this is why the prayers of this set of partners were going unanswered. The solution? Commit to a consistent prayer time, each and every day, and commit to being open to having this Prayer Partner experience change your life. This person checked back with me several months later and said that commitment and consistency had made all the difference.

Today I remain committed and consistent in my
spiritual journey.

Day 39 . . . Letting Go

Have you noticed that the hardest thing for us to do sometimes is to let go? We want what we want, when we want it, in the way that we want it! Control helps us to feel like nothing "bad" is going to happen to us, and that we can somehow avoid unnecessary pain. And some level of control in our lives can be a good thing. But many of us will take it to extremes, treating Life as an errand boy who is only here to satisfy our demands. Life doesn't work that way. Life wants us to let go and let it work through us to give us the greatest possible experience. For that to happen, it requires us to stay open and flexible and in a state of possibility. This is where our Prayer Partnering helps us; it's like a daily reminder to do what we need to do, and leave the rest to God.

Today I let go and let Life lead me.

Day 40 . . . Freedom from What Binds You

Many Prayer Partners wonder what to pray about. Should they pray for something specific (e.g., a job, a relationship) or for some quality of being (e.g., peace of mind, patience)? Either will work, but we often ask people to look at where they feel they are being held back in their life, or even being imprisoned. Then we ask them how it would feel if that were no longer in their life. Most of the time, they state that if they didn't have whatever it was that binds them in their life, then they would feel more free, happier, and the quality of their life would improve. Work with your Prayer Partner to find the right prayer for you that will help bring you more freedom. You can choose many things to pray about, but none may be as important as praying for freedom from whatever is holding you back.

Today I know that nothing and no one can hold me back. I am free.

Day 41 . . . Staying Connected

The Prayer Partner experience is unique in that you and your partner come together for a very specific reason: prayer. You aren't there to talk about your date last night, or a television show, or to complain about your boss. This relationship has a very special and holy purpose—to connect you both to your Infinite Source within. Developing the habit of daily prayer with your partner can make a connection between you two that can potentially change your lives. Treat your

Prayer Partner time as if it were one of the most important things you are going to do each day. Why? Because it is!

Today my connection to my soul is full and clear. I listen to what my soul is telling me.

Day 42 . . . The Game of Life

Does life seem chaotic sometimes? It can feel as if there are no rules, no guidelines, just catch-as-catch-can. The good news is that there are spiritual laws of the Universe that are as absolute as the law of gravity or other scientific laws of the physical universe. (See the book *The Kybalion* by Three Initiates for more on spiritual laws.) Spiritual laws are true for all people, at all times, and you can learn them, use them, and as you get practiced in them, you can rely on them. It's never the law that doesn't work; we don't always correctly use the law. Praying daily is a way to access and enact those spiritual laws in your life, and use them to let your larger life emerge. You can use these spiritual laws for material things, for healing, or for greater understanding. The more you use them, the better you become at using them, and the more you will see the positive results reflected in your life.

Today I play the game of life and win!

Week 7 Exercise

Answers sometimes come more readily when we ask the right questions. Questions are keys that serve to unlock wisdom that is deep within. You can use the power of questions with your Prayer Partner to help you both make some deep inner discoveries. And by asking questions aloud, with your Prayer Partner, you are—as with your prayers—maximizing the power of the questions, and therefore the answers.

Try this: Take a few minutes during one Prayer Partner session to ask each other some questions. Ask your partner an open question, and then practice active listening as they answer. Then you each take a breath, and have your partner ask you the same question in return. Your partner should also practice deep listening as you say your answer. Take another breath, and then ask another question and repeat the process. It may help to write down several questions ahead of time, or choose from these questions:

- How can I open more to Life?

- What do I need more of in my life?

- What is Life asking of me right now?

- What do I need to know from my soul today?

- What, if anything, am I resisting?
- What, if anything, is stopping my flow within?
- Whom do I need to forgive today?
- Whom do I need to ask forgiveness from?
- How can I give and receive more love today?

Let these questions become gateways to understanding and revelation. The well of wisdom is always available to us, at all times, and never more so than when we are in prayer. The answers will reveal much about where you are in your life, what you want more of, what you want less of, and what is needed of you by Life at this time. How amazing to have a Prayer Partner who can share with you their truth, and also be a witness to yours.

Day 43 . . . Peace in My Heart Brings . . .

Many of us would like to change the world. We would like to bring positive change to the entire world, such as peace and prosperity, which would erase poverty or the need for wars. What is the best way to change the world? Begin with ourselves! We can, as Gandhi said, be the very thing that we wish to see in the world. One person who truly and authentically becomes something great will bring about more change in this world than a million people who just talk about it. Each morning we can choose to live these spiritual teachings more fully than the day before. Each prayer we utter can be a reminder to live the words rather than recite them. Whatever we desire in this world can be. Let us each lead the way.

Today the peace in my heart brings peace to my life and the world around me.

Day 44 . . . Gratitude List

Here's a great question for you: how many things are you grateful for in your life? Somewhere on this page, or on another piece of paper, or in your journal, make a list of everything you can think of that you are thankful for. There are probably some things that are obvious, such as friends and/or family, a home, or even life itself. As you make the list, you'll no doubt begin with those areas that are most apparent in your life. But as you keep writing, challenge yourself to see beyond the obvious to things that you might not usually think to be grateful for. One of my lists a few years ago included indoor plumbing (because it was snowing outside and I remembered that my father used to tell about the outhouse they had on the farm he grew up on), a song that I had heard on the radio that inspired me, and also the wind chimes outside my bedroom window that always made beautiful noises that lulled me to sleep. You can be grateful for anything and everything, and the more you are grateful for, the more you will be blessed with.

Today I am grateful for everything in my life.

Day 45 . . . Staying Positive

We are what we believe. The more positive thoughts we have, the more our life will reflect that positivity. But staying positive can sometimes be a challenge. The television broadcasts scary stories 24/7, the newspapers try to dramatically get your attention through frightening headlines, people love to spread negative gossip, and on and on. Staying positive in this often negative world can seem so hard. One excellent solution? Your daily Prayer Partner experience is a way to mentally and emotionally rise above the level of fear and confusion to a higher place. From this higher point of being, you won't ignore what is going on in the world; but you will be able to be more effective in it. You can choose a positive perspective, and that positive perspective will affect the way you experience your day.

Today I choose to be positive all day long and experience everything in a positive way.

Day 46 . . . Pure Joy

What would your life be like if you experienced more joy today? Would you be more productive? More content? More energetic? More . . . ? Joy is a vital ingredient in creating a life that is worth living. Many people go through days or weeks or even years with little or no joy in their lives. They exist rather than truly live. How can we add more joy in our lives? Make a list of what brings you joy, big or small. Your list might include activities, people, music, travel, good food, and a zillion other things. That is the place to start. Spend a small amount of time each day with one thing that brings you joy. You will be creating an expectation and habit for more joy, and in turn you will experience more joy. If you are not experiencing much joy in your life, bring this into prayer with your partner. Pray for more joy, starting today.

*Today I see and experience pure joy all around me
and within me.*

Day 47 . . . Showing Up

The first rule of grasping any opportunity that will improve your life is first to show up. If you want a more toned body, you must first show up to exercise. You don't get a toned body by wishing for it; you get it by doing exercises that will create it. The more you exercise, the better your results will be. This is true on the spiritual path as well. Whatever it is you are praying for in your 90-Day Prayer Partner Experience is more easily obtained when you show up consistently, morning after morning, with your Prayer Partner. You'll be amazed at how your life will change when you begin to show up for prayer. You'll also grow more confident the more you show up each morning. Why? Because the more you show up, the more you'll see the results of your prayer experience.

Today I show up. I am spiritually aware and awake all day.

Day 48 . . . Prayer Is an Endless Resource

Do you know that all of the spiritual power that was available to Jesus and the Buddha and every great spiritual master is also available to you? And not only that, it is available to you right here, right where you are sitting, right now. That spiritual power is available at all times, everywhere, to all people. The more we know this, the more often we will draw on this power in our lives. Think about it for a moment; you may even want to close your eyes and ponder it. This limitless resource, the entire power of the Universe, is available to you right now. You need only draw on it. How? Start by asking God, during your morning Prayer Partner prayers, to show you how to use this power, and how it can positively use you!

Today I draw on the limitless resource that is
available to me at every moment.

Day 49 . . . Om Sweet Om

The word "om" is a Sanskrit word that invokes a feeling of adoration and completeness. It has been used as a mantra by countless millions over centuries; it is a word and a feeling that brings wholeness to life. It also is considered to be a "perfect sound" when uttered aloud. Prayer Partnering is similar in that the prayers you pray with your Prayer Partner can bring praise and affirmative completion into your lives. Each open and positive prayer we pray is perfect, whether we pray it aloud or silently. Whether or not you actually use the word "om" in your meditative prayer time, your Prayer Partner experience is a time to bring that spirit of "om" into your own life. We are linking to the energy of Life's wholeness. Does it take practice? Of course, but the practice is part of the joy-filled journey that is our 90-Day Prayer Partner Experience.

Today I invoke the spirit of "om" in my life.
I am whole and complete.

Week 8 Exercise

Throughout time, people have used various methods to inspire and help each other. Letters, books, Scripture, music, and even art are all ways that have been used to inspire other people. Spiritual directors assign spiritual readings for monks or nuns to read daily, to keep them uplifted and on track. In the Middle Ages, troubadours created short songs that would express a positive message to a group of people. Whatever the method, the intention is to impart inspiration, and the result is inspired people.

We live in an age in which there are countless ways to connect with others in inspiring ways. Using modern technology to this end may seem new, but it really is following in a time-honored tradition.

What does this have to do with your Prayer Partner? This week make it your mission to inspire your Prayer Partner in creative ways. Send a daily e-mail with an enlightening quote, or an encouraging prayer that you wrote, or a motivating passage that you copy out of one of your favorite books. Use the social network Web sites (such as Facebook or Gaia or MySpace) to connect with your Prayer Partner, and send them messages to lift them up. You can Twitter these inspirational messages so that your Prayer Partner (and others) can get the message. Download your favorite positive songs and burn a CD for your Prayer Partner.

Whatever you do, and however you do it, keep the same intention in mind. This is a week in which you are letting your Prayer Partner know that you are holding them in the High Watch of spiritual love. You are seeing the Divine, and knowing for them that the positive outcome to their prayer is on the way to them. Your mission this week is to bring about a strong and tangible connection so that your Prayer Partner is reminded daily that the Universe loves and supports them . . . and so do you!

Day 50 . . . Do the Basics

When we begin to use the spiritual laws and see results in our lives, it is easy to think that we could "graduate" from the practices that have helped us and begin doing more complicated and "deeper" practices. But the spiritual masters throughout history have attained their highest enlightenment by using the basic spiritual practices over and over throughout their lives. They may have added to the basics, but they never stopped using them. Thinking that there will come a time when we won't need prayer is like saying there will come a time when we won't need to exercise to stay healthy, or even that we won't need gravity any longer. The basic spiritual practices invoke the laws of the Universe, and our Prayer Partner experience helps us to use these laws more and more effectively in our lives.

Today I remember that as I believe, so it is done in my life.

Day 51 . . . Surrender

One of my favorite hymns has a line that I love: "I'd rather fight You [God] for something I don't really want, than take what you give that I need." The point is that we sometimes try to hold on and control and force and overpower and compel and push and shove our life, and we can feel the results of that in our exhaustion and our anger and our fear. This approach to life might work for a while, but it cannot work in the long run, and it will not work if you want to have any kind of true serenity in your life. There is a great ease in letting Life gently move us forward, sometimes slowly, sometimes quickly.

We are always asked to create a vision, participate in its coming true, but not have to do it all by ourselves. Take a breath and know something very important: you do not have to do it all by yourself. You need only do your part. What is your part? Usually your part is the part that brings you the most joy.

Today I surrender the "lesser" and "smaller" in my life, and allow myself to live all that Life has in store for me.

Day 52 . . . Dreams

What are your dreams? Do you actively try to live them, and when you realize one of them do you immediately go for the next? Or do you hide your dreams away in secret? Do you take steps to help make them come true? Or do you just wish and hope they will, and talk a lot about them but not actually do anything? One thing I've learned over the years is that we are given dreams, and we are given the means and the passion for these dreams to come true. It's amazing how often we accept so little for ourselves when there is so much available to lift us up, to help us. If you have a dream (or dreams), do not accept anything less than that dream in your life. This is your life, and the responsibility for how you live it is yours. Will you choose to move toward your dreams?

I (and your Prayer Partner) both believe you will!

Today my dreams become realities.

Day 53 . . . Focus

Ernest Holmes once wrote, "There is a power for good in this Universe greater than you, and you can use it." What he meant is that when we harness the energy of our desires, we are like an unstoppable force. The key is to focus our energies and attention on those desires. Start with one thing you want to see manifested in your life, and put all of your attention, passion, energy, and awareness on this one thing—not just for one day, or one week, or even one month. Do this for as long as it takes for this desire to manifest in your life. Once it does, choose again, and then again. Eliminate activities or thoughts or habits that hinder you from realizing your desire, and replace them with those that further it. You can have what you want, and focus is the key. Bring your focus each morning to your Prayer Partner and then follow where you feel led.

Today I am focused, attentive, and aware.

Day 54 . . . What Stands in Your Way?

When we pray for something, we either get what we want, or we get what stands in the way of our getting what we want. If we want more love in our life, for example, we will either get more love, or we will get more experiences that are anything but loving. These experiences do not happen to tell you that you don't deserve more love. Instead, these experiences are there to show you where in your life you need to practice more love. These experiences are perfectly designed for you to give more love, which in turn opens you up to receive more love. When you pray for something and seemingly the opposite shows up in your life, remember to rejoice that Life is showing you exactly where you need to change in order for your desire to come true.

Today I will pay attention to what
Life is showing me.

Day 55 . . . Giving Up the Lesser

Our life is filled with thoughts and beliefs and actions. What is interesting is that for the most part we have the ability to think and believe and act as we please. What astounds me is how often we choose to think such small thoughts, believe such small beliefs, and do such small actions. If I were to walk up to you on the street and hold up a $1 bill, a $1,000 bill, and a $1,000,000 bill (all three legit bills) in front of you, and I were to tell you that you could have any one of the three you wanted, which would you choose? Most likely you would choose the largest bill. We have that same choice with our thoughts, beliefs, and actions. Are you choosing $1 thoughts/beliefs/actions? Or $1,000,000 ones? Or something in between? Your Prayer Partner time can be a great place to learn to give up the lesser in your life and embrace the greater.

Today I trade in the smaller experience in life for a greater experience of my life.

Day 56 . . . Higher Altitude

Recently I was flying from the city where I live to another city, where I was scheduled to give a talk. Shortly after we lifted off the ground, the plane ride became extremely bumpy. The pilot's voice came over the loudspeaker to let us know what was going on: "Folks, we've run into a bit of turbulence, which is normal as we move to a higher altitude. Once we get to the level we are going to, the ride should smooth out." Our lives work the same way. As we are moving from one level to another we might experience some turbulence. We can either stay in the turbulence, or we can move to a higher spiritual altitude, and our journey will become smoother. Prayer is a method of going "higher" spiritually, a way of rising above the turbulence in our lives so that our ride is smoother.

Today I move to a higher altitude and experience a smoother ride.

Week 9 Exercise

Time to meet again with your Prayer Partner in person, if possible. Turn back to the exercise for Week 5 and follow those instructions.

What is interesting is to see how your experiences and answers to the questions you ask each other will have both remained the same and changed from your answers of just a few short weeks ago. Make note of where you are now, what has changed, what has not changed. Finally, each of you might take turns stating an intention for how you want the rest of your 90-Day Prayer Partner Experience to go. Would you like more focus on the praying time itself? Would you like to add some other elements to the prayer time? Do you want to change the prayer or keep the same one?

You have just a few weeks left, so use this opportunity to map out what would be the best outcome for you both. This will help to inform your remaining Prayer Partner sessions.

Day 57. . . Deep Rest

We all do so much. Between our families, work, school, e-mails, bills, responsibilities, commitments, and so much more, it can all feel overwhelming. It's important to remember that a very important part of our lives is rest. There are different levels of rest, but what I'm talking about here is deep rest, the kind that you can get only from stepping away from life—even if it is for just one day, or longer if possible—and letting yourself just "be." Let yourself rest all the way until you feel it deep inside. Often it will be my Prayer Partner who will remind me that it is time for me to take a deep rest break. When I take a deep rest, I continue to do my Prayer Partner work, as I have found that daily prayer during my time of rest helps me to stay centered on resting, rather than doing.

Today I rest deeply and am renewed.

Day 58 . . . The Gift of Blocks

What blocks you from your good? What stands in the way of you and what you want in your life? It is the very things that block us or keep us stuck that can be our greatest teachers and our greatest tools for transformation. What has been the biggest block in your life? What has that block prevented you from experiencing or having? How has that block kept your life smaller than if it (the block) hadn't been there? What, if any, were the benefits of having this block in your life? Finally, is there any way that this block can actually help you rather than stop you? If no immediate answers come, don't force them. Instead just stay in an open expectation that everything that you need to know about any and all blocks in your life, and how they can be transmuted from stumbling blocks into stepping-stones, will be revealed at just the right time, in just the right way.

Today I am open to seeing any "blocks" as stepping-stones.

Day 59 . . . Energy Follows Action

The formula by which I live my life is this: energy follows action. We may want something to happen or change or improve in our lives—healing, love, peace, abundance, and so forth—but all the wanting won't actually make anything happen. We may think that we'll be more generous once we make more money, but using the equation "energy follows action" we find that we'll make more money once we're more generous. We may want love, but it can't come unless we are more loving. Whatever you want more of in your life, begin by taking an action first. Bring your desire into your daily morning prayer time so that you can open yourself up to guidance from the Divine about the exact right action to take.

Today I take positive action toward what I desire in my life.

Day 60 . . . In the Valley

There is a natural rhythm to life—ebb and flow. Peaks and valleys. We will find ourselves in a valley from time to time. The "valley" might be a depression, or illness, or a dramatic life change, or even a discontent with how things are going. Whatever it is that has brought you to your valley, you can relax and know that the valley is part of the process of life. Being in this place is not wrong, and it does not mean you are doing something incorrectly. What it does mean, however, is that this is a time for you to stay very focused on moving forward, and also to be very attentive to what Life is trying to say to you. Usually our "valley" experiences are there to help us let go of something, or to change course. Trust yourself and trust Life. Keep walking through the valley, and you will make it through to the other side.

Today I walk forward and keep on moving.

Day 61 . . . Abundance

Here's an interesting thing: the Universe is limitless and filled with an abundance of everything, yet many (if not most) people walk around as if they have very little and are always wanting more. There is a song about this that states that we often are "standing knee-deep in a river, dying of thirst." Where is the abundance that is already in your life? Where is there prosperity that you might be already experiencing but are ignoring? Here's another interesting thing: the more you see abundance in your life, the more you will experience more abundance in your life. Jesus told us this truth in the book of Matthew when he said that to those who have a lot, more shall be given, but for those who don't have, all will be taken from them. He meant that an attitude of abundance will attract more abundance in your life, while an attitude of lack and poverty will attract more lack and poverty in your life. Use your Prayer Partner experience to develop an ever increasing awareness and appreciation for the abundance that is already in your life. And then notice how that mind-set will bring you even more!

Today I see abundance in my life everywhere I look.
Thank you, God, for everything.

Day 62 . . . Spiritual Support System

When I bought my last computer I also bought the ability to call and speak to the computer support group, who could (theoretically) answer any question I might have about the computer, and who would be there to help me if something should go wrong. This service is something I don't mind paying for, because I tend to be challenged when it comes to computers, and these computer services have usually been helpful in the past. I know that I can call and get the answers I need. Think of your Prayer Partner as a spiritual support system that you can plug into and draw on whenever you need or want help. This system is there to provide and offer help in connecting deeply to the Source of Life in your life. Your daily prayer acts as a call to the Source, and you will get answers. The answers generally come in the form of a feeling, a hunch, an experience, or something similar. Unlike the service for my computer, which was quite costly, your Prayer Partner doesn't cost a thing, and you will get perfect results.

Today the Source of Life supports me at every moment and at every step.

Day 63 . . . Saying Yes

Do you say yes to Life? Or do you tend to say "no, thanks" when Life has a change in store? Do you tend to be open and receptive to change and new ideas for your life? Or are you more cautious, or maybe more suspicious, and only want to move forward when you feel safe and secure? There is no right or wrong answer to these questions, but your answers will help to remind you where you are, and how much you trust Life. The more we trust, the more we tend to say yes to any positive opportunity Life throws our way. The less we trust Life, the more suspicious we are about the outcome of any change, and sometimes we even decide that no change is safer than saying yes to Life's opportunities. The more we pray, the more we see how much the Universe wants us to succeed. We learn we can trust It and begin to say yes as we go along. The struggle between what we want and what we're afraid of gets smaller and smaller.

Today I say yes to life, and Life says yes to me.

❧

_____

_____

Week 10 Exercise

An old saying states: "The Universe abhors a vacuum." When there is an empty space, the spiritual masters have taught for centuries, Life moves in to fill it. If we are not aware of this natural law, we won't know that we can help to direct the filling of that space, and if we don't take any action the space often gets filled with something we don't want. But once we know that this is a way that Life works, we can participate by cocreating what goes into this vacuum.

One excellent way to create a positive vacuum in your life is to add a small period of silence to your daily Prayer Partner time. Spend two or more minutes during your daily prayer time in silence. This is not a structured, meditative time, or a time when you read inspirational literature; this is literally a time when you and your Prayer Partner are sharing the silence. One of you should keep track of time, as sometimes we can get blissfully lost in the silence. Just "be" together in silent solitude. You might be surprised at how powerful silence is with another person.

At the end of the short silent period, speak your daily prayers aloud. State your intentions, and pray as you have been doing during your Prayer Partner experience.

By adding the period of silence, both of you are literally creating a sacred space that sets the stage for a positive filling of any vacuum that arises. And by immediately following that sacred silent time with your prayers, you are stating your intention of how you would like that vacuum filled. In other words, you are literally creating a space for your desires to be born into your life experience.

Silence might be the most potent spice you can add to your Prayer Partner experience. It's like the advanced, express course to manifesting your prayers. Remember to take time for gratitude during your prayer time, and also remember to ask your partner for extra support and offer the same to your Prayer Partner during this time. Communicate with your Prayer Partner what your experience is of how this silent time helps prepare the way for positive developments in your life.

Day 64 . . . Choice in Every Experience

In every experience that happens to you, you have a very important choice to make: you get to decide what the experience means to you. Every experience can be seen in many different ways. To one person a divorce might mean shame, or failure, or a fearful experience of loneliness and anger. To another a divorce might mean freedom, or rebirth, or even relief. Some people will choose to hold grudges for the rest of their lives, while others will learn to forgive. Who decides? Who makes those choices? You do for yourself. One exciting aspect of the Prayer Partner experience is that we are starting each day with an awareness of what is holy and what we are grateful for, and by starting the day in this way we tend to make healthier and more positive choices, both about what actions we take and about how we choose to feel about what happens to us.

Today I choose to see everything in my life through the lens of positivity.

Day 65 . . . Your Soul Has a Message

We've mentioned before in this book that Life is always trying to talk to you, that there is always something that is trying to be revealed to you, and through you. Your soul, that perfect essence within, is always wanting to encourage you, help you, bring you solace and comfort, and urge you further on down the path. How can we hear Life? What does the voice of our soul sound like? Unlike in some sacred texts, where God reveals himself in dramatic ways as with the burning bush, our soul tends to be more subtle than that! Life will speak to us in the form of thoughts, or coincidences, or ideas that excite us, or hunches, or strong feelings, or many other such ways. I even had a profound spiritual breakthrough while I was listening to the lyrics of a song that was playing on the radio—it seemed to be aimed right at me (I know it wasn't, but it felt that way). Your Prayer Partner experience is a way to hone the skill of listening to Life, hearing your soul. Listen today!

Today the message of my soul is loud and clear and I listen to what it has to say.

Day 66 . . . Don't Give Up

I remember trying out for a sports team as a child. The idea of playing the sport seemed so fun! But after the first practice, which was exhausting, I decided I wanted to quit. Playing was harder than I thought, and I could tell that I would have to practice a lot to get good at it. Looking back I can see that I wanted the experience of playing this sport well without actually putting in the practice to make that happen for me. We can be like that as adults sometimes as well. We want to be a famous author, but when we see all the hard work required to write a brilliant book and find an agent, we never get past page 10. We want lots of money, but we don't want to do the work of getting out of debt and learning how to be excellent stewards of the money that we do have. We want to lose weight, but we give up after a week when we have a craving or don't want to exercise. Those who get what they want are those who don't give up. Stay committed to your Prayer Partnering and see how it will transform your desires into realities!

Today I move forward tirelessly and steadily.

Day 67. . . Answered Prayers

Some of my prayers, prayed with my Prayer Partner, were answered in surprising ways. One of my Prayer Partners prayed for unconditional love from a man. She prayed this prayer for quite a while. At one point she felt the inner urge to begin volunteering at a hospital, and through that experience she began to work with orphaned children. She found she had a particular connection with one child, a little boy who just lit up every time she walked into the room. She began to spend more time with this little boy, and at one point she decided that she wanted to adopt him. "Your prayer was answered," I told her. "What do you mean?" she asked. I told her that she had prayed for unconditional love from a man, and here he was—just a littler man than she was expecting. She was overjoyed to see her prayer answered, but then said, "Next time, I'll be more specific!" She began praying again, more specifically. End of story? She ended up marrying one of the social workers who assisted with her adopting the little boy. The prayer was answered, just not in the way she thought it would be.

Today, I know that all of my prayers are answered,
and I pay attention so that I don't miss the answers!

Day 68 . . . Here I Am

One of the best spiritual practices we can engage in is called "Adsum," which is a Latin term which is translated as "here I am." Our Prayer Partner experience is a way that we can move out of an awareness of "gimme gimme" to one of openness to every possibility. We sometimes don't know what is best for ourselves, or we often ask for so little in our lives. When we pray with an attitude of "here I am," we are placing ourselves under the guidance of a Universe that loves us and is constantly trying to give us more of what we need and desire. The prayer "here I am" is a way of saying that you trust the Universe, and that you know and expect your highest and greatest good to happen. Begin your prayers with "Spirit, here I am" and end them with "Adsum."

Today, Spirit, here I am. Adsum.

Day 69 . . . Try Something New

It is easy to get stuck in a rut. We can get very comfortable by doing things a certain way, every day. Sometimes we don't even know we are in a rut! What can we do? Every now and then, decide to try something new during your Prayer Partner experience. Add in a song, or read a poem, or say your prayer in a different room, or go outside. By trying something new you are adding an element of change. Like any change, it may not feel comfortable at first, because it isn't what you are used to. That is exactly the point: it isn't what you're used to. It might be better than what you are used to. It might be different from what you are used to. It might make your prayer time more interesting, or deeper, or more exciting. You don't have to necessarily try something different every day, for there is also value in a consistent practice, but by adding something new now and again, you are saying to Life that you are willing for something new and wonderful to happen in your life.

Today I am open to trying new things and experiencing life in new ways.

Day 70 . . . Maximizing Each Moment

A relative of mine celebrated his ninetieth birthday recently. We had a little party for him, and I asked him what piece of advice he would give me. He didn't even pause for two seconds when he looked me in the eyes and said, "Every day, realize that there is no time to lose." He went on to tell me that he couldn't believe he was already ninety and wondered where the time had gone. There was so much he had wanted to do in his life, he said with some regret in his voice. The way our life works is that we are given life only one day at a time. Just today. And so you have one day—today—to live life as fully as you can. There are two possible days you can have today: one where you get by and live on automatic pilot, and another in which you live fully and choose to live in the joy and wonder that is available all the time to each one of us. It's your choice. Which will you choose?

Today I choose to live my day fully and freely. I am alive!

꧁❀꧂

Week 11 Exercise

We are all sensitive to many factors in the world around us. Many of us are finely attuned to the sounds and noises that surround us, and we can direct these by either surrounding ourselves with music or sounds that we love, or minimizing sounds that we don't. Many of us also are finely attuned to smells and have used aromatherapy to enhance our spiritual experience. I believe we all are finely attuned to visual beauty as well.

Where are you when you do your daily prayer time with your Prayer Partner? Are you sitting on a couch in the living room? Or do you have a little corner of a room in which you've placed a pillow to sit on when you pray? Or do you sit at the kitchen table? There is no right or wrong place to be when you do your daily prayer—as long as it is reasonably quiet—but by making wherever you pray more visually stimulating, you can add depth to your prayer experience.

There are many things you can do, depending on where you sit now. Here are just a few ideas that might be useful:

- Buy (or make) a special chair that you use only for prayer time.
- Make a little altar that you look at while you pray.

- Create a "prayer chest" in which you can literally put your prayers (written on slips of paper).

- Sit in front of a window so you are looking outdoors.

- Sit or walk outdoors to be in nature during your prayer.

You can surround yourself with candles, incense, chimes, statues or other art, pillows, photos, sacred texts, or anything that inspires you. I turned an entire small room (more like the size of a large walk-in closet) into my own private prayer room and decorated it lovingly so that every time I walked into that room the room itself put me immediately into that centered place.

We cannot live without beauty: our souls yearn for it. So adding beauty to your Prayer Partner time will only help to feed your soul and in turn improve your entire experience praying with your Prayer Partner, and beyond.

Day 71 . . . Secret Project: Inspiration

What we give away comes back to us. This is a basic spiritual law of the Universe, and we see it in action all the time in our lives, especially as we become more sensitive and aware in our Prayer Partner time. What if today you went on a secret mission for God? What if you decided that you were a secret agent and your mission was to spread inspiration wherever you went? You could target people at work, or at school, or on the street, or in your family—whomever you come across during the day—and give them a dose of inspiration. Studies prove that one positive encounter can positively effect a person's entire day; the reverse is also true: one negative encounter can negatively effect a person's entire day. For this one day, decide in your prayer time that you are going to cause as many positive encounters as you can. You will be doing two things. First, you will be helping people to begin having a positive day, which in turn will help them spread their positivity to others, and so on. Second, you will be helping yourself to have a positive day. This is a very important secret mission from the Divine: will you say yes?

Today I choose to be an agent for positivity in this world and in my life.

Day 72 . . . He Ain't Heavy . . .

Why is it that we can sometimes see the great potential that lies in other people more than we can see it in ourselves? It is a gift to be able to see the potential and the highest good for our Prayer Partner, even more than they might be able to see it for themselves. It doesn't cost anything, hurt anything, and it never feels like a burden to see the Divine truth within your Prayer Partner. To alter the song a little, he ain't heavy, he's your Prayer Partner! Your seeing their best within them raises the vibration of their own belief—just as their seeing the best in you raises your own belief. Julia Cameron, author of the beautiful book *The Artist's Way*, calls these "believing mirrors." You can be the believing mirror for your Prayer Partner, and they for you. What would you do today if you knew that there was someone who totally believed in you and the potential of the Universe to act positively in your life? And what would your Prayer Partner do if they knew that you believed the same for them?

Today I see the Divine best within and for my Prayer Partner.

_____

_____

Day 73 . . . No Vacations

One Prayer Partner surprised me one day. I had told him that I was going on vacation to a foreign, tropical paradise, so I wouldn't be able to talk to him all that week. "Don't they have phones where you are going?" he asked. Sure, I told him, but I needed to take a vacation. "A vacation from praying," he said. "Why would you want that?" It took me a minute to let that sink in, but I saw that he was right. Why would I want a vacation from prayer? What would I be taking a vacation from, exactly? A great life, more awareness, joy and ease in my life? No, he was right: prayer was the very thing that would make my vacation more meaningful and restful, not less. We ended up praying every day of my vacation, despite being on different continents in different time zones, and it blessed us both in countless ways. I was praying each morning on my cell phone while walking along a fairly deserted beach, the ocean and sun surrounding me, and I was able to bring that beauty and ease to our prayer time. The result? We both ended up having profound spiritual experiences that week.

Today I choose to pray and connect to my Good, no matter where I am.

Day 74 . . . Pay Attention

Life is constantly talking to us, trying to communicate to us where it wants us to go, where our treasure lies. But we often walk around preoccupied with to-do lists and feeling overwhelmed. Or we get caught up in feeling bored and lost. Either way, we are avoiding listening to and seeing what Life is trying to tell us. Your Prayer Partner time is a way to fine-tune your listening skills so that you can hear Life whispering in your soul, urging you toward your great good. It is this deep listening to Life that we can learn to access from our Prayer Partner time, and the more we do it, the more we live from our center rather than from our frazzled, hectic self, or our confused and inactive self. The act of paying attention to our own life, and to Life itself, is one of the greatest gifts you can give yourself.

Today I choose to listen to Life.

Day 75 . . . In the Flow

We are always invited to be in the flow of Life. We are always able to access that flow in our lives. When we do, we are in tune with the Infinite, our lives run more smoothly, we experience synchronicities and positive experiences, and we end up living our best life now. But so few of us consciously allow ourselves to be in that flow. It takes time and practice to live in the flow, and that is one of the benefits of Prayer Partnering. You are tuning yourself into that flow, so that it might flow to and through you. You are opening yourself so that the flow can take you new places, ever greater and more fulfilling. Every day you pray with your partner, you are moving into the flow, which is flowing toward your greatness.

Today I am in the flow of life and follow where it leads.

Day 76 . . . Persistence

Every spiritual tradition and every spiritual master has said the same thing, albeit in different ways: you must be persistent in your quest for spiritual wisdom and understanding. Read any sacred work and you will find that it encourages you to practice the spiritual persistence every day. Jesus said that we must "die daily" to the old and be "born again," which means to leave behind the lesser and begin each day anew in the awareness of our Divine nature. The Talmud says that we must act "ceaselessly daily," and Rumi encourages us to spend each day of our lives learning to "dance" with the Divine. The Hindu and Buddhist sacred works, as well, encourage a commitment to daily practice. Why? Because as we open ourselves up to the Infinite Life each day, we grow in profound ways, and we get to learn and express our purpose here on this earth. Make no mistake; your Prayer Partner experience is a substantial spiritual practice!

Today I choose to be made anew and alive in my spiritual awareness.

Day 77. . . Letting God Speak through You

A few years ago I had to attend what I knew was going to be a difficult business meeting. The other people in the meeting were upset and had been confrontational about their position. Needless to say, I was not looking forward to this meeting. I decided to call my Prayer Partner and bring this meeting into prayer, knowing that the highest and greatest good for all parties would happen. And my Prayer Partner said something outrageous; he prayed that my meeting would be "transformative and even joyful." When he said those words I thought he was crazy. Didn't he know this was going to be painful? But as I walked into the meeting later that day I remembered his words and prayed a second silent prayer: "God, please speak through me so that this meeting is transformative and joyful for all of us." A peace came over me, and I found myself saying to these businesspeople, "How can we make this a productive meeting so that we all leave here happy?" Just opening up the meeting with that expansive question shifted the entire mood of the room. Not only did we all end up getting what we wanted, but we also brainstormed as a group on some new projects that were lucrative and exciting. We all left the meeting transformed and joyful. Bring everything into prayer, and then let go and let God speak through you.

Today I let go and let God speak through me. I turn over everything to the Higher Power.

Week 12 Exercise

This is the twelfth week in the 90-day cycle—the penultimate week during which many people lose their steam. For whatever reason, many people drop out at this stage of the process. Some are afraid of getting what they want, and they see how prayer is bringing it to them, so they quit. Others self-sabotage by dropping out, saying that since they haven't gotten what they were praying for yet, this whole process doesn't work. Still others don't make any adjustments to their prayer time with their partner, so they get bored and stop praying. Whatever the reason, if they don't focus their attention and stay open to Life, they will find that it is harder to get what they desire.

This is a good time for you to reflect—either with your Prayer Partner or in your journal—on how you are feeling so close to the end of this 90-day period. Anxious? Excited? Frustrated? Peaceful? Energized? Whatever your feelings are, let them be.

Don't judge them, and don't judge your Prayer Partner's feelings, either. What you can do, however, is look at what you need to do during this week that will support you and make your prayer time joyous and spiritually fulfilling.

For ideas, look back over the previous weeks' exercises and see which ones appeal to you. Or brainstorm with your Prayer Partner on some other ideas. Or spend time reflecting, see what ideas come to you, and record them in your journal.

These last two weeks are often the most memorable of the entire experience, so make sure you have the support of your Prayer Partner, as well as anything else you need.

Day 78 . . . Giving and Receiving

If you've ever watched ballroom dancing, you know that the partners are dancing a highly choreographed set of movements that are totally in sync with each other. The sacred texts tell us that Life works that way as well. As we take each step, Life moves in perfect rhythm with us. The Law of Compensation states that each action is perfectly reflected back to us, just like a choreographed dance with the Divine. As we give, we receive perfectly. As we withhold, we are withheld from. As we love, we are given love perfectly. As we withhold love, love is withheld from us. It is a perfect dance, and one that we are cocreators in. Think of your Prayer Partner as your dance partner as you learn to dance through life, learn the steps of making the most positive choices, choosing the highest thoughts. Together you will dance through your lives, seeing how the Divine is always in step with you. The dance of life is beautiful!

Today I choose to dance with the Divine.

_____

_____

Day 79 . . . Lift Up Thine Eyes

What do you do when you don't know what to do? The Bible has a quick and effective solution: lift up thine eyes. What does this mean? It means that in every situation in which you want to have a different experience, choose to see the situation in a different way. You can't get the answer to a situation from the same level of understanding that created it. Lift up thine eyes means to lift up your awareness so that you see the situation in a new and "higher" way. How do we do that? Bring it to prayer. Prayer is a way of elevating our awareness so that we can see our life and everything in it the way that God sees it. When we are in the forest, we can't always see where we are going or how what we are experiencing fits into the whole picture. But as we lift up our spiritual eyes, we can see the whole forest, where we are in it, and where we need to go. Prayer is a way to go higher and to see more.

Today I lift up my spiritual eyes and I see where I am and where I need to go.

Day 80 . . . Who Are You Today?

We all have ideas and beliefs about who we are, and many of those ideas and beliefs are fixed in stone. We know what nationality we are, what race we are, what political party we support, what music we like, what religion we are, and on and on. We sometimes get fixed in these ideas of who we are, and we don't allow ourselves to be anything else. What if by being so sure of who you are, you are missing out on who Life wants you to be? What if by being so fixed on being who you think you are, you are choosing less for your life than Life would choose for you? That doesn't mean we have to throw out those associations. But it does mean that in our prayer time we can ask Life to tell us who It wants us to be. You may be surprised at how much Life has in store for you, how big Life would like you to live, how much Life would love to give you if only you were open to receive it. Let go of who you think you are and become authentically who you truly are.

*Today I am God's creation. I let God mold me and
shape me into the person God would have me be.*

Day 81 . . . Thank You, God, for Everything

Go back and read the story on pages 121–123. This is an insightful story about seeing everything in your life—both the seemingly good and the seemingly negative—as the same, so that you can be open to Life bringing you what you need. We can always choose to see every situation in a new way, a way that helps us rather than makes us a victim. Many of history's greatest leaders, whether in politics or religion or the arts or even sports, have communicated a similar message. What they at one point thought was an obstacle or hardship in their life ended up being a great lesson or motivator or blessing. They used each experience as spiritual fuel to take them further. That is part of what made them stand out in history: the fact that they were able to see and use every experience to challenge them to live more fully. What is in your life right now? How can you bring everything in your life to prayer, so that you can not only give thanks for it but see that everything that is in your life right now can serve you?

*Today I thank God for everything, and I have no
complaints whatsoever.*

Day 82 . . . Building Your Spiritual Muscle

A while back I joined a fitness boot camp. This was an intense exercise program, and we were outdoors doing these difficult and challenging exercises every morning, rain or snow or sunshine. At first I thought it was too hard for me, and that I wouldn't be able to do it. I decided to give it two weeks, and if at the end of two weeks I couldn't do it, I would quit. After the first week I was tired from waking up so early, and so sore I could barely walk! During the second week, however, I found that what seemed impossible in the first week was suddenly a bit easier—not easy by any means, but I had already improved just a little. I was surprised that I would see improvement, even just this little bit, so quickly. Now, after being in the boot camp for many months, I can do so much more than I ever thought I could. Each step toward mastery—which is ongoing—came by my showing up daily and doing all that I could do that day. Your Prayer Partner experience works the same way. Showing up daily and then letting the experience seep into your very being might be hard at first, but after a few weeks and then months you will see the results clearly and surely in your life, and in your Prayer Partner's life as well. You are building spiritual muscle each and every day.

*Today I know that I am growing stronger and
stronger in my spiritual mastery.*

Day 83 . . . Let It Be

Recently at a church service I was surprised that the choir sang a gospel-tinged rendition of the Beatles' classic song "Let It Be." I was further surprised when I found myself crying as they chanted, "Let it be, Lord, let it be," over and over again at the end. Something within me was resonating with the message of letting things be as they are, not trying to change everything, not trying to "push the river," not trying to do or to be anything other than what I was in that moment. I mentioned this to my Prayer Partner the following morning, and it moved her as well. As the Bible reminds us, there is a time for everything. Sometimes it is time to strive and move, and sometimes it is time to stop and rest. In all times, at the end of each day, we can look at the day and "let it be." Tomorrow we will begin again.

Today I let it be, Lord, I let it be.

❦

Day 84 . . . What Does My Prayer Partner Need of Me Today?

It's easy to focus on ourselves, especially in our prayer time. What do we need today? What do we desire for our lives? Where would Life have us go today? These are all good questions to ask of ourselves, but during our daily Prayer Partner experience there is another good question to ask: what does my Prayer Partner need of me today? Or another way of putting it: how can I support my Prayer Partner today? It might be enough just to pause and mentally send them loving thoughts. It might be that you will feel moved to send them an encouraging e-mail, reminding them of the Divine truth of their lives, lest they forget during the busyness of the day. It might be that you call them and tell them that you are holding the High Watch for them that day. Or it might be saying a simple, short prayer for them several times throughout the day. Whatever it is, supporting your Prayer Partner is a beautiful act of service. And one that is being reciprocated as they serve you as well.

Today I support my Prayer Partner and know the highest and greatest good is true for them right now.

Week 13 Exercise

You are now coming to the end of the 90-Day Prayer Partner Experience. Whether this is your first 90-day experience or your tenth, you'll no doubt be ending the 90 days in a different spiritual (and maybe emotional or even physical) place than when you began it. Prayer takes us on journeys, and the journeys are always unique. The more we work with a Prayer Partner, the more we learn to recognize the soul's language in our life, and learn how to be responsive to it.

After the last day of the 90-day period, make a date with your Prayer Partner, preferably in person. If you are able to meet in person, celebrate this cycle and bring it to a natural close. You might choose to meet for a meal, break bread with each other, and discuss the entire Prayer Partner experience. You might go do something fun, such as take a walk in the park, or go on a nature hike together.

If you are not able to meet in person, you can still make a date over the phone. Choose a time when you won't be interrupted for about an hour minimum. You may want to choose a different time than the morning time when you pray.

Either way—in person or on the telephone—use this time to congratulate each other on completing this commitment. Ask each other what has changed, what hasn't changed, and what you learned from the experience. Also ask your partner if they felt supported, and how they could have felt even more supported by you.

Another good question to ask is whether or not you want to continue on as Prayer Partners. I've had people who have been my Prayer Partner for one 90-day period, and others who have been my Prayer Partner for years at a time. It's up to you both, what works best for you. All along we've been encouraging you to take these Prayer Partner ideas, use what works, and leave what doesn't. This is especially true as you contemplate your next Prayer Partner. If you feel you are finished with this Prayer Partner, then thank them and let them know you are ready for a different Prayer Partner now. If you want to continue with the same Prayer Partner, ask them if that would work for them as well. Don't take it personally if someone you want to work with wants to move on; you want to pray with a Prayer Partner who wants your exact qualities. If it isn't the partner you've just completed the 90-day experience with, the next perfect Prayer Partner will be on the way.

However you decide to move forward, we encourage you to continue your daily morning prayer time. As you've no doubt seen and experienced in the last 90 days, beginning your day with prayer is one of the most powerful and important spiritual tools you have available to you. As one of the devotions pointed out: prayer can be your first resource, not your last resort.

Day 85 . . . "Treat and Move Your Feet"

There is a saying in many spiritual centers about prayer, which is sometimes called "spiritual mind treatment." They will say about every prayer (or treatment) that is said, "Treat and move your feet." What does this mean? The treatment is an affirmative prayer that is said. To treat and move your feet means to say your prayer and then take whatever action comes to mind toward the answer of the prayer. It means that we cocreate the answer to our prayer with the Universe, and therefore we are responsible for our part of creating the answer. We are only responsible for our part, not necessarily the whole thing, but we cannot desist from doing our part. Many times people want prayer to be like magic: they say a prayer and then sit back and think they don't have to do anything. But Life always wants to involve us in everything, and we are made from Life itself. God isn't a waiter who waits on us; God is within you and is cocreating your life experience with you, to the degree to which you will cooperate. Pray and then listen. If an action is revealed to you, do the action. Through this practice you are doing your part in the prayer process.

Today I pray, listen, and act.

Day 86 . . . God's Hands

Mother Teresa once said that it wasn't her hands that made anything possible; it was God using her hands that made everything possible. When we realize that we are made by the great Creator, we can also realize that everything that we do is the great Creator acting in us and through us, as us. Our hands can be the hands that God uses to lift someone up, or to create a work of art, or to write a song, or to save a life (maybe our own). Our voice can be the voice God uses to speak words of love to someone who needs to hear them, or to speak peace in a situation that seems chaotic, or to sing a song that reaches deep into souls. Our feet can be the feet God uses to go where there is a great opportunity that will bless us greatly, or to walk where there is someone who needs our support, or to run in the direction of our bliss and joy. Our mind can be the mind that God uses to think of solutions to problems big or small, the thoughts that God can use to reach the heart of someone whose heart is aching, or the mind that understands that there are no limits to life. Being a Prayer Partner opens us up to being a vessel that God uses in infinite ways, to bring Light into the world.

Today I am a vessel of God.

Day 87 . . . Three Feet from Gold

Studies of people who desire to lose weight are fascinating. These studies show that when people join a weight loss group or program, a large number of them will not finish the entire program, and there are two junctures at which most of those people will drop out. Some drop out shortly after beginning. They just don't have the commitment to go beyond the first part, and usually they drop out because they wanted the program to be easier and they wanted to lose weight with very little effort. Others drop out right near the end of the program, shortly before they reach their weight goal. They run out of steam and don't reach within to take themselves all the way to the end. They literally give up right before they get what they want. Napoleon Hill, author of *Think and Grow Rich,* calls this stopping "three feet from gold." You and your Prayer Partner are nearing the end of your 90-Day Prayer Partner Experience together.

Keep going, keep praying, keep believing. Don't stop three feet from the gold in your life.

Today I choose to keep on keeping on.
I reach for and grab all the gold that Life has in store
for me.

Day 88 . . . Lifestyle Now

Earlier I wrote about joining a fitness boot camp and how difficult that experience was at the beginning. The boot camp runs on three-month cycles, and you have to sign up again for each three-month cycle. At the end of my first three-month cycle with the boot camp I was so pleased with the results I had experienced that I immediately signed up for the next three-month cycle. Now I can't imagine living without some excellent form of exercise, a tool to stay healthy and strong. The same is true with Prayer Partnering as well. The first time I did a 90-Day Prayer Partner Experience I loved the results and immediately wanted to do another 90 days with my Prayer Partner. Now it has become a way of life, and I can't imagine living without this powerful form of spiritual connection, a tool for staying spiritually healthy and strong. The more you do it, the more it does for you and in you.

Today I stay the course, and I know every prayer I
speak is answered.

Day 89 . . . Where Two or More Are Gathered

Jesus was clear: wherever two or more are gathered in His name, there He would also be. Another way of saying this is that when you and your Prayer Partner come together with the highest of intentions, you will be lifting your awareness to its highest place. It is from this high place that you can experience more of Life, you can choose the highest choices, and you can have the greatest effect in the world. You are doing as Jesus instructed and as Jesus practiced; you are moving on up from a lower place of limits and distractions and the lesser, to a higher place of limitlessness, focus, and infinite possibilities. Every day we have a choice of where we want to set our intention. When you and your Prayer Partner are praying together and lifting each other higher and higher, you are accessing that spiritual power that Jesus also accessed. You are taking Jesus at His word when He said that those things He did, we also can do, and even greater. You are not just saying words with someone else each morning; you literally are tapping into the entire potential of the Divine and letting it flow through you.

Today my life reflects the unlimited spiritual potential of the Divine.

Day 90 . . . Starting Over Again

Congratulations on finishing your 90-Day Prayer Partner Experience! You and your Prayer Partner have stayed the course, prayed many prayers, and lifted your awareness to new heights. Both of you no doubt have had a unique and exciting journey. Now is the time to reflect on all that this experience has meant for each of you, and how it has changed your thoughts, your actions, and your experience. It is also time to start again. Prayer is not just something we do from time to time, just like water is not something we drink only when we are parched. We drink water throughout the day to hydrate our bodies, to get the benefits from this amazing liquid, to stay healthy, and even to stay alive. There will never come a day when we won't need water anymore, or when we will be "beyond" drinking water. It's the same with prayer. We can make prayer part of our life every day so that it is like spiritual water, always nourishing us, keeping us spiritually healthy and spiritually alive. Prayer is the living water of God; it is the well where we find our connection to all that is Divine. Take this time to complete your 90-day journey well, and to turn around and choose prayer once again.

Today is an ending and a beginning.
I choose to choose the living waters of prayer as my
connection to the Divine in my life.

APPENDIX A

Prayers for Every Day

Following are ten affirmative prayers that we have included on a variety of topics. Please feel free to use these prayers during your Prayer Partner time, or any time. Also feel free to change or alter any of these prayers so that they are tailor-made for you. Each affirmative prayer is written in the first person plural so that you and your partner can "know" the prayer for yourselves.

Prayer for Health

We come together as Prayer Partners knowing there is only One Source of Life, and that Source has created all Life, including the life of my Prayer Partner and myself. This Source is perfect, whole, and complete. There is nothing that hinders this Source, nothing other than the perfection of Life itself. We align our thoughts with this truth right now, that we are one with the One that created us. And it is in this awareness that we align ourselves with the truth that perfect health is ours, that we are divinely guided to everything and everyone who can help us in perfect health, and we are open to every thought and experience and revelation that brings perfect health to us right here and right now. We are the image of perfect health, and we claim that as our truth now. Perfect health is mine, and perfect health is my partner's. As we lift our minds to this truth, we in turn lift our bodies and our very lives to this truth. We know that the Universe supports us, and we follow where Life leads us. Health is ours, and we give thanks to the Source itself for this truth. We release this prayer now, completely, knowing that even as we release it, it is true. We say "yes" to every way this prayer is answered, as we say "yes" to Life.

And so it is . . . Amen.

Prayer for Balance

Divine Power exists everywhere and is available at all times. This Divine Power is the creative power that has created the heavens and the earth, and all life. Right now we bring ourselves together in the spirit of this Divine Power, knowing it to be all-powerful in all ways. There is only this one Divine Power, and it shines through us now. We completely and fully bring our awareness to this shining truth and now choose to experience It right now in our lives. With Divine Power comes perfect and complete balance of all things. Balance of love and peace, of yin and yang, of rest and activity. There is a balance as the natural order of all life, and this balance is now the natural order of my life and the life of my Prayer Partner. Our inner life conceives and receives this balance as our natural state, and therefore our outer life also reflects this balance. All is good, whole, and complete in our lives. From this moment on anything that we experience that seems out of balance we now know is only part of our life rearranging itself so that balance can be ours. We love this truth and we believe it now. We accept balance as our life, and now we breathe in balance and breathe out balance. We give great thanksgiving for this natural state of balance, which is restored and made new in our lives. Thank you, God, for bringing about full balance in our lives. We now release this prayer to You, knowing it is done and balance is restored.

And so it is . . . Amen.

Prayer for Joy

The Eternal Giver of Life is always present, always creating. This One Presence, which is God, is forever singing the song of joy in this Universe, creating only like Itself. Since the Eternal Giver of Life is pure and complete joy, the truth of all life is that it is created with joy, and by joy. Joy is the quality of the Eternal Giver of Life that is ours right now. My Prayer Partner and I are both created in the image and likeness of God Itself, and as such we were born with the seed of joy in our hearts. This seed has now flowered, producing a life of joy in every way. We experience joy in our health, in our relationships, in our life mission, and in our every action. Joy is our way of experiencing the Eternal Giver of Life in our lives, and we choose joy in every situation. We choose to see joy underneath any disguise, and we choose to see the joy within every person and experience. Our joy spills over into our realization that joy now is easily ours. And it is with great joy that we give our thanks to the Eternal Giver of Life, and we allow this prayer to be our truth now.

And so it is . . . Amen.

Prayer for Life Direction

There is but one Creator, which is God the Almighty. This one Creator is perfect harmony and right action. It is an ever-knowing Creator, which continues to create like Itself, therefore it continues to create perfect harmony and right action at all times. This creates constant movement forward and constant growth. Within this one Creator is all life, including my life and the life of my Prayer Partner. The one Creator is operating within me and my partner now, in absolute perfection and love. We need only allow the Creator to speak in our heart, and we will follow where It leads. As the Creator sings in our souls, we move forward with each breath. Every day I become more confident that I am divinely guided and led in the exact right direction for me, so that I might live a richer, more satisfying, more creative life than ever before. I know this for my Prayer Partner as well, that this same One Creator pulses through their lives as well. It is all one Life, and we are living it fully and completely. We go forth with a complete trust that all direction to our greatest life is given clearly, and we say "yes" to all opportunities. We live in a state of gratitude for this truth and allow it to happen naturally and effortlessly.

And so it is . . . Amen.

Prayer for Abundance and Prosperity

Within myself and my Prayer Partner I now accept as truth that we were created by the Infinite Source of all Life. This Infinite Source, which is forever creating, is the only power and presence there is. There are not two powers in this Universe—for how could there be an infinite source and something else? There is only this one creative power, and It creates out of Itself all Life, and all is like Itself. That Infinite Source creates an infinite supply that is available to all, including me and my Prayer Partner. This supply is never-ending, always available, and constantly flowing. We ourselves control the flow of the infinite supply in our lives, and today we allow this flow to increase freely. As it is in my heart, so it is done in our lives, so I speak my word now for both myself and my Prayer Partner that we now ask for and receive a full measure of God's goodness unto our faith, and even more. The divine promises of infinite supply are now made manifest in our lives, and we joyously and happily accept them as our own. Prosperity of all kinds now floods into our lives—abundance in our thoughts, our being, our love, our relationships, our health, our material well-being, our peace, and our joy. Anything and everything that would obstruct our good from coming to us is now erased, and replaced with the guidance and acceptance of all that the Father has in store for us. Thank you, God, for your never-ending supply of good that is Your pleasure to give, and Your great joy for us to receive.

And so it is . . . Amen.

Prayer for a Soulmate

We enter into the sacred circle in our hearts and minds. We focus on the truth that there is one supreme power in the Universe, and that power is God, Spirit, Divine Flow, the One Mind. This One Mind is the originator of all, the Creator, the Architect of life itself. There is no opposing power to the One Mind, which is all-powerful, all-knowing, and everywhere present. By entering this sacred circle I am knowing—for myself and for my Prayer Partner—that we are completely immersed in this One Mind. The One Mind is who we are, and it expresses Itself as us. From this aware-ness we know that all things are possible. We know that every desire is placed in our heart by the One Mind for a purpose. We bring into this sacred circle the desire for the perfect soulmate, knowing that as this desire is expressed, it is also made manifest by the very One Mind that cre-ated the desire. We both focus our spiritual attention on this beautiful desire, knowing that the very soulmate, with the very qualities that sing in my soul, is now come into my life. Two complete and whole souls coming together for a deep and intimate connection—I know now that this is the truth of my life, that my soulmate and I have found each other at the exact right moment, in the exact right way. I am loved thoroughly and I love freely. Thank you Life for this experience of Love, which I now embrace and express with every breath. Love is mine, and I am grateful.

And so it is . . . Amen.

Prayer for Forgiveness

For all those I have harmed, knowingly or
   unknowingly, I am truly sorry. Forgive me and
   set me free.
For all those who have harmed me, knowingly or
   unknowingly,
I forgive them and set them free.
For the harm I have done to myself, knowingly or
   unknowingly,
I am truly sorry. I forgive myself and set myself
   free.

A Prayer When Going through Difficult Times

We are embraced in the heart of the Living Presence, and enfolded in the Infinite Love. Together we come together to know that this heart of the Living Presence beats inside our very lives. We are the heartbeat of God, and God's heart beats in us. This heartbeat is the rhythm of Life, moving us forward through all experiences. We move forward confidently, knowing that we are always connected to the Divine, we always have resources available to us, and we are guided to our greater good at all times. All stumbling blocks turn into stepping-stones. Everything that appears to be a barrier transmutes into a help. There are no obstacles to my good and the good of my Prayer Partner. I now choose to know and believe the truth, which is that all is well. Thank you God for this truth, and for always leading us to higher ground.

And so it is . . . Amen.

Prayer for Love

The great Love of the Universe is with me and my Prayer Partner right now. This Love is the Love of eternity, the Love that created all life, the Love that we are made of. This Love is the very essence of who we are. As the revelation of Divine Love floods our minds, we lift our thoughts and expectations to Love itself. We are love, we give love, and we receive love. Love is at the heart of our thoughts, words, and actions, and we bring love to every person and experience we encounter—including ourselves. The more love we give, the more love we receive. We do not worry about love, for Love finds its own, and it has found me and my

Prayer Partner. Thank you, Love, for being who I am, and for attracting to me more love than ever before.

And so it is . . . Amen.

Prayer for Overcoming Fear

There is One Power in this Universe, and It is a power for good. This One Power is infinitely mighty, and eternally all-knowing. There is only the One Power, and I allow that knowledge to fill up my very being. It is who I am, and it is who my Prayer Partner is as well. We are one in the One. All feelings of fear disappear as I know this truth. Anything that gave me fear or apprehension is gone when I know and feel the strength of the One Power within myself. What is there to fear but my mistaken belief that there are two powers in the Universe—God and something else? I do not believe that now, and I move forward confidently knowing that the One Power is my power now. As I know this for myself, I know it for my Prayer Partner as well. Fear no longer has command of my life. Instead Life moves me and my Prayer Partner both forward in the right time-space sequence. What I thought was fearful is transmuted into an opportunity. With gratitude we release this truth to the Universe, knowing it to be true for us both.

And so it is . . . Amen.

APPENDIX B

The Three Secrets of Answered Prayers

The Prayer Chest, our first book, is about being open to receive all of life's riches. In the novel a notebook is discovered hidden within an ancient prayer chest. The notebook contains three secrets to prayer. Although *The Prayer Chest* is a work of fiction, and the prayer chest described is meant as a symbol of our faith—our willingness to turn within for help in times of trouble—the three secrets to answered prayers are not fiction. We've included this section as a way of explaining how answered prayer works.

The three secrets to answered prayer are profoundly true.

What follows is an excerpt from the book that provides an excellent explanation of how to remain more open to receive the answers to your prayers.

I introduce you to the Secret of the Prayer Chest in the way that Grandma Mary did me—through questions that invite reason rather than response, my son.

Grandma Mary began thusly:

"Since the beginning of time every man and woman has prayed—hundreds upon thousands of prayers daily. Why then are only a handful answered?

"Is it a person's goodness that determines it, or his piety? Perhaps his cleverness or his generosity to the old and infirm? If it is goodness that determines it, why are the prayers of unkind and selfish men answered?

"Even the deepest thinkers have not found the final piece to the puzzle of prayer—why some prayers were answered and others not—and this, as you can imagine, weighed heavily on the mind of man."

Stone by stone, dear Joseph, Grandma Mary laid the foundation of her argument.

"After living in the mystery of unanswered prayers, generation after generation, it proved to be an unbearable frustration to mankind. Man wanted peace of mind, even a false peace would be better than this frustrating and fruitless pursuit.

"Here then, Malachi, is what mankind agreed to believe so that the search for the elusive answer might come to an end: It is God's Will that chooses which prayers are to be answered and which are not.

"Look and you shall see, Malachi," she said with a leaden sadness, "how this belief at once calms you, yet robs you of your capacity to have your prayers answered. "Slip one hundred prayers into the chest and do not use the secrets of the Prayer Chest and all one hundred shall go unanswered. Slip one hundred prayers into the chest using the secrets of the Prayer Chest, and every last one shall be answered—to the utmost.

"The Prayer Chest returns to mankind the authority to have our prayers answered and use that authority as we wish."

The First Secret of the Prayer Chest:

Prayer Is Answered through You

When you talk you are a dam overflowing, but when you listen you are an open vessel ready to receive.

Reluctantly I disclose to you that I was such a man whose words spilled over. Like a drum I banged my prayer into God's head in an effort to help God remember.

The Second Secret means write your prayer down once and talk no more of it to God. From that point forth listen. Only listen.

"And where," I asked Grandma Mary, "might a farmer like me with chores to do from sunrise to sundown find time to listen?"

"Return to your work, do what you must, but with a part of you ever inclined toward listening. Know that God speaks to us continuously, but we cannot hear if we do not listen."

That God must work so hard to get our attention wrenches my heart, my son.

The Second Secret of the Prayer Chest:

Prayer Is Answered When You Listen

If you have applied the first two Secrets, you will by now have noticed your faith increasing as well as tests to your faith. Bid them both welcome for both are signs of progress.

This is the meaning of the Third Secret, my son: from the instant you slip your prayer into the Chest, everything that comes to you is a portion of the answer to that prayer.

Do not make the mistake that mankind makes when it throws open its arms to growth or good fortune alone and rejects all else. Doing so leaves one lopsided, like a cart with wheels on one side only.

"We must learn from Nature where opposites walk hand in hand," Grandma Mary said. "Look how effortlessly Nature shifts from day to night, season to season, releasing each in its turn."

Mankind is not like this. We choose gain over loss and light over dark, and by refusing half, we are no longer able to receive the whole of our answered prayer.

My son, make yourself ready for loss and letting go, as perhaps, part of the answer to your prayer. It may not be immediately apparent how failure leads to flourishing or loss fertilizes the ground for gain, but trust that it shall.

The Third Secret is the greatest test of our faith, and it is precisely at this point where most men fail. That is why on the precious few chance encounters that found us alone together, Grandma Mary would whisper this to me—part prayer, part advice—lest I forget, "Be like an ocean that refuses no river."

"Through an open vessel," she explained, *"prayers flow unobstructed, and heaven finds an inlet and outlet through which to reveal itself on earth."* Here, then, my son, is how:

The Third Secret of the Prayer Chest:

Prayer Is Answered When You Welcome Everything

The Three Secrets of Answered Prayer

Prayer is answered **through** you.

Prayer is answered when you **listen**.

Prayer is answered when you **welcome everything**.

ABOUT THE AUTHORS

Founder and Spiritual Director of Sacred Center New York for over eight years, **August Gold** is also an award-winning author and has served as an inspirational teacher and counselor in New York City for twenty years. She speaks nationally and internationally at conferences and organizations.

Joel Fotinos, a vice president at Penguin Group (USA) Inc., is the publisher of the Tarcher imprint and founder of the Putnam Praise publishing program. A cofounder of Sacred Center New York, he is ordained New Thought minister and lives in New Jersey.

You can visit them on the web at:
www.augustgold.net
www.joelfotinos.com

HAMPTON ROADS
PUBLISHING COMPANY

. . . for the evolving human spirit

Hampton Roads Publishing Company publishes books on a variety of subjects, including spirituality, health, and other related topics.

For a copy of our latest trade catalog, call (978) 465-0504 or visit our distributor's website at *www.redwheelweiser.com.* You can also sign up for our newsletter and special offers by going to *www.redwheelweiser.com/newsletter/.*